© 2018 Jamie C. McHugh

Jamie C. McHugh
The Best of Luck

All rights reserved. No part of this book may be reproduced or transmitted in any form or by any means, electronic or mechanical, including photocopying, recording or by any information storage and retrieval system without written permission of the publisher, except for the inclusion of brief quotations in a review.

ISBN-10: 978-0-2285-0127-5 (Paperback)

ISBN-13: 978-0-2285-0130-5 (e-book)

Distributed by:

Jamie C. McHugh
www.thebestofluck.biz
jamiecmchugh@gmail.com

This book is dedicated to my parents
who nearly named me

Lucky.

The Best of Luck

JAMIE C. MCHUGH

TABLE OF CONTENTS

SECTION ONE
BEGINNING YOUR LUCKY JOURNEY

Introduction: Getting Started on Your Lucky Life

Chapter 1: Lucky Journey

Chapter 2: Appreciating Your Luck

Chapter 3: It's All in the Name

SECTION TWO
ATTRACTING LUCK TO YOU
MINDSET AND HABITS

Chapter 4: How to Make Lady Luck Smile Upon You – Attracting Luck to You

Chapter 5: Lucky Habits

Chapter 6: Discovering the Lucky Habits

Chapter 7: Healthy Body, Healthy Mind, Healthy Bank Account

Chapter 8: Old Habits Do Die Hard

Chapter 9: Team Luck – Goal Setting

SECTION THREE

ALL KINDS OF LUCK

Chapter 10: Are We Born Lucky? May Luck Be With You

Chapter 11: Good Luck or Bad Luck

SECTION FOUR

Chapter 12: Earth Luck – Feng Shui

SECTION FIVE

Chapter 13: Lucky Charmers

Chapter 14: Lucky Charms

Chapter 15: Lucky Travel

Chapter 16: Happy Go Lucky

Conclusion: Make Tomorrow Your Lucky Day

Section One

BEGINNING YOUR LUCKY JOURNEY

INTRODUCTION

GETTING STARTED ON YOUR LUCKY LIFE

> Patience and perseverance have a magical effect
> before which difficulties disappear
> and obstacles vanish.
>
> JOHN QUINCY ADAMS

Do you feel you lead an unlucky life? Do you avoid the number 13 or walking under ladders? Are you ill all the time? Unemployed or underemployed? Is your love life non-existent? Did your life partner vanish along with your luck?

Most days, do you long to wake up lucky? Or wish for luck while drinking your first cup of coffee or tea in the morning? Is luck not in your tea leaves? Well, look again. Look very deep into that cup, because luck is there. You control it. You can find it. You can create it.

Things not going your way? Planning on winning the lottery? Hoping for a big inheritance? Hopefully, one of those last two windfalls will come to you, but you shouldn't count on it. This book may not help you win the big one, but it can help you on your way.

By the way, most lottery winners end up blowing the money. Why? Because they didn't build in intention. They didn't have a mindset designed for success. Most winners don't have a platform. The bad habits they had before are now magnified. When that million is gone, they consider themselves unlucky.

Are you still reading this book? That must mean you want to lead a lucky life. Lucky you. Welcome. The minute you picked up this book, you already started creating your luck. This book was designed to help you become the source of your new, auspicious life. You are responsible for the things that happen in your life. You will be the fount of your luck. I created this book to be a reference for people like you; people who want to take charge of their lives, people who strive to be among the favored fortunate, people who perhaps suffer from "down on my luck" syndrome.

Many of us know about Oprah Winfrey's story and how she never gave up through sexual abuse and teenage pregnancy. Oprah persevered, completed high school, earned a scholarship to college, and of course, worked her way up through the television ranks to become a superstar.

But did you know that Jim Carrey and his family lived for a time in a van in a relative's yard? Carrey was forced to drop out of school to take an eight-hour a day factory job to make ends meet. But Jim did not let that stop him from pursuing his career.¹

Jim Carrey and many other successful people did not just wake up successful one day. Steve Harvey, Halle Berry, Daniel Craig, and Jewel were all homeless at one point, sleeping in cars, on benches or on the streets. Research the humble beginnings of many other accomplished people and you will find a common theme: hardship, desire and perseverance.

Johnny Cash grew up during the Great Depression. His house did not have glass in the windows. During the winters, his mother hung blankets to keep out the cold. Cash's brother was killed in a sawmill work-related accident. Johnny never forgot his upbringing, which became part of his greatest hits.

Shania Twain was born into a struggling family in Ontario, Canada. Sadly, Shania's mother and stepfather were killed in a car accident when she was only twenty-one. Shania was the oldest of five children and needed to support the family. Shania did this by singing at local resorts until her siblings were old enough to care for themselves. Shania then set her sights on Nashville.²

Michael Jordan's career wasn't a slam dunk. As a fifteen-year-old sophomore, he was only five feet ten inches tall and could not yet dunk a basketball. As a result, Jordan did not make the varsity team. Michael decided to turn the cut into motivation and he became the star of the junior varsity team. When he made the varsity squad, his work ethic didn't drop off. You know the rest.

Michael J. Fox was diagnosed with Parkinson's when he was just twenty-nine years old and at the peak of his career. At first, Michael was depressed and turned to alcohol. However, he changed his mind set and became an activist for Parkinson research.

Bill Gates' first business failed. Albert Einstein didn't speak until he was four. Stephen King's first novel was rejected many times, as was J.K. Rowling's first Harry Potter novel.

A Wrinkle in Time, written by American writer Madeleine L'Engle, won the Newberry Medal, the Sequoyah Book Award, and the Lewis Carroll Shelf Award and was runner-up for the Hans Christian Andersen Award. This book, rejected at least twenty-six times, is now a major motion picture.

Jack Canfield, the creator of the First Chicken Soup for the Soul, persevered through 144 rejections. Yes, you read that correctly. 144 rejections. Jack Canfield had a significant purpose, ambitious goals, and grit.

As you read through this book, you will notice a few quotes by Dr. Seuss. While Dr. Seuss wrote for children, his sage advice rings true for many adult life situations. Dr. Seuss's story is another one of tenacity. **His books were not a success from the beginning.** Twenty-seven publishers rejected his first book; however, Dr. Seuss went on to win several major awards, including two Academy Awards, two Emmy Awards, the Laura Ingalls Wilder Award and a Peabody Award.

Perhaps you have heard of Kyle Maynard. Kyle is a motivational speaker, bestselling author and an award-winning mixed martial arts athlete. These are not Kyle's only achievements. Kyle was born with the rare condition known as congenital amputation, which prevents the development of fetal limbs. Kyle became the first quadruple amputee to ascend Mt. Kilimanjaro. If you ever feel down on your luck and motivation, read more about Kyle.

In the pages ahead, you will read other stories of determination, steadfastness, and staying power. There will be scientifically tested theories about believing in luck. You will learn ways and means for increasing your success. These narratives are here to show you how to reach your desired objectives. Use these ideas and actions to expand your repertoire of lucky tools. Whether you feel you are fortuitous or not, let this book show you the path to manifesting a favored, fortunate life.

Do you aspire to be a movie star? A T.V. mogul? A prosperous entrepreneur? Do you want to feel like you are a lucky person? Do you wish to attract love or the right people into your life? Do you desire to not only dream about a magnificent future but to make an excellent future happen? Are you a person who wants to be so fortunate you can go out into the world and make the world a beautiful place for others? If you believe you indeed are a lucky person, you can increase your good fortune.

I'm glad you decided to come along on this odyssey. Perhaps you are a person who already works hard, who puts forth a strong effort on a daily basis. You are out there getting things done. Your life is fine, but not as supercharged as you would like it to be. Perchance you are looking for that extra bit of luck; those extras steps to guide you to the next level. I wrote this book for you.

Maybe you are someone still looking for your path, wondering what the next step should be. Mayhap life is entirely going your way at the moment and you are looking for your way into the garden of clover. I also wrote this book for you.

A Google search of the word "Luck" suggests that it may have entered the English language as a gambling term. Is your luck something on which you are willing to gamble? If not, let's get you started on your way to a lucky life.

SECTION ONE

This first section is where you'll begin your journey; you'll reflect on the luck you already have.

You will give thought to your life, your name, your luck and count your blessings. You may say, "Thank goodness I purchased this book. I feel so lucky already."

If you are looking to start a family, still trying to determine your career path or get or gain success at a job, this section is for you.

With excuses to Lady Gaga, "You were born this way."

SECTION TWO

In this section, you will 'examine' the lifestyles of the favored and famous: their traits, mindsets, and habits. This segment is where you will learn how to form new patterns and reset your old, unwanted habits. You will set goals and explore methods to help you achieve your intentions.

To help you put your new, lucky life into action, at the end of some chapters you'll find a *Lucky Learning* section which highlights each chapter's salient points. A few of the chapters will also provide a personal page for you to journal your newly acquired, leading-edge wisdom.

SECTION THREE

This section is the area in which you will explore various types of luck. You will ponder if you or others around you were born lucky. Have you overcome terrible luck? Was your bad luck good luck? You will read how determination helps us handle adversity.

SECTION FOUR

Do you want to know a secret of millionaires and billionaires? Explore this section to learn more about Mankind Luck, Earth Luck, and Feng Shui.

SECTION FIVE

Section V is a diverse section, a medley of happy, travel, and charming luck.

You will learn to become happy and lucky. Journey through this section to seek how to increase your lucky mindset via travel.

CHAPTER 1

LUCKY JOURNEY

The day you decide to do it is your lucky day.
JAPANESE PROVERB

I was born Lucky. Or nearly so. When I was born, my parents almost named me Lucky. My folks were very young and destitute, with no money to pay the hospital bill. The hospital would not release my mother and I until the bill was paid. Luckily, on the third day, my father, who was selling stocks and bonds, made a huge sale. And so, I was considered Lucky.

Throughout my life, there were times when people commented that I was very lucky, Was luck omnipresent? Assuredly not. Despite having been born 'lucky', I was not born into a favored life. My parents' life was a financial struggle. My father was blind until advanced technology made surgery possible. We lived in what today would almost qualify as 'a tiny house.' While we never went hungry, food staples included tube steaks, baloney and Klik. Throughout this, my parents were determined my sisters and I would get a valuable education and a laudable job.

I did achieve this goal, with many struggles, but also with help from my companions: persistence and grit.

Grit is defined as courage, resolve and strength of character. Lucky people are resilient. They turn problems into challenges. Auspicious persons see the gift; they see the blessing not the burden. Much of one's success is due to the voice within. Those who traipse through life complaining they are so unlucky are focusing on their woes, their tribulations. Negative, 'unlucky' people blame external factors, bad luck or the environment.

In my condo there is a window ledge next to a doorway. On that ledge is a plaque that reads: *If You Are Lucky Enough to Live at the Lake, You are Lucky Enough.* As you step through that doorway a majestic view of a shimmering sapphire lake greets you. This is what a lucky life means to me. Of course, there are the other worldly goods and non-material possessions most of us would agree on: family, health, a good job, etc. We all desire something unique that makes life special for us. What is your lucky dream?

One day I happened to walk past a poster that was advertising classes in a unique life area. At that moment something came over me and I immediately registered. Over the next few weeks, as a result of what I was learning in these classes, I made a number of small changes in my life and my living arrangements. During the following months, my life began to change significantly. People began to ask under what lucky star I was born. Curious as to what occurred? Read on to find out. I promise to reveal the secret of this course and many more tips to help you change your luck.

Before we continue on your lucky journey, let me introduce you to Mr. and Mrs. Lepp, affectionately known to their friends as Mr. and Mrs. Leprechaun. Mr. Lepp was teased most of his life because of his name. Not only did his surname sound like leprechaun, but Mr. Lepp also looked somewhat like a leprechaun. Having been born late in the year, he was one of the youngest in his class, so he was a tiny guy for the early part of his life. Mr. Lepp had a wee bit of Irish ancestry in him. While his hair wasn't flaming red, it was somewhat reddish. More like carrot red. Yes, poor Mr. Lepp had been bullied during grade school. However, as the birthdays continued, Lady Luck smiled upon Mr. Lepp and he grew tall and strong. As in all good fairy tales, the handsome prince met the conquering, clever princess. The Leprechauns have been married for ten years and lead a lovely, lucky life. After years of practice and hard-work, Mr. Leprechaun, Arthur, became an exceptionally successful sculptor and painter who prefers to go by the name Art E. Mrs. Lepp, Carolyn, is an entrepreneur. She has a flourishing e-commerce business with a highly ranked Instagram account.

Once upon a time, way back when, while Mr. and Mrs. Leprechaun were dating and were still just Art and Carolyn, they were offered a sweet chance to go to Ireland to housesit. The catch was, they had to decide quickly. The pre-arranged housesitter had to cancel due to an emergency. The house owner was committed to a long-term business trip and needed someone immediately. There were dogs and cats and goats and ponies and, oh my, who would take care of them? Well, Art and Carolyn had never taken care of goats and ponies, but they were sure they could learn. Art could paint and sculpt anywhere. Carolyn had been thinking about a new opportunity for a while and thought this might be just the boost she needed to take a leap of faith to start her own business. The Lepps had been a wee bit concerned about being lonely. How would they make friends? Could they make friends? Maybe they could take classes - particularly one on raising goats and ponies. Volunteering might work for them. What a lucky chance! Art and Carolyn accepted the offer, grabbed onto their lucky shamrocks, booked a flight on Clover Leaf Air and off they flew.

Let's peek in on Mr. and Mrs. Leprechaun. Art E. is gazing out his condo kitchen window onto a busy city street. It is an ordinary city street with crazy traffic, a kaleidoscope of pedestrians and the accompanying noises. Regardless, Mr. Leprechaun appreciates the cherry blossoms bursting forth on the trees planted on the boulevard and the delightful, blue morning sky. While enjoying the outdoor scenery, Mr. L. is also slowly sipping a glass of lemon water. Mrs. L. is nearly finished getting dressed for her morning work-out. She has completed her morning meditation and is planning to work from 8 a.m. to noon, as is her regular habit. As a final touch, she slips many multi-colored bracelets onto her right arm and heads to the kitchen.

Anticipation is building under the toadstool. Art and Carolyn have one child named Robert (Bob) and are now excitedly awaiting the birth of their daughter. But what to call her? Carolyn loves flowers and wanted to name her daughter Rose or Heather, but the Lepps were savvy enough to do some research. No flowery little Leprechauns in their humble castle. Alexandra, maybe? Curious what the research says? All is revealed in Chapter 3.

A lovely, little fairy-tale, you say. *"But what does this have to do with my luck? I don't want to go to Ireland to raise goats."*

Perhaps you don't want to go to Ireland to raise goats or any animal for that matter. Possibly you don't want to travel to Ireland at all, or to any other country. Quite likely you love where you live and are content.

What is your fairytale? What do you want to achieve? What is your dream? What habits, traits, and strategies will you learn and incorporate into your new auspicious life to realize your fairytale?

Here is your challenge. By the end of this book, your luck will have changed. You will be able to identify all the lucky traits and strategies the Lepps incorporated into their lives to help them accomplish their fortunate fairytale life.

CHAPTER 2

APPRECIATING YOUR LUCK

> The secret of getting ahead is getting started.
> MARK TWAIN

It is time to get started on your road to a vibrant, lucky life. Now is the time to start designing your new, charmed life. Step up, get up, look around your home or go outside to look. Find three things for which you are thankful. A family member, your children, a photo from an unexpected trip you took, a cherished item, healthy food in your cupboard, glorious roses in bloom? Aren't you lucky to have all those pleasing belongings and special people in your life? Do this every morning when you first get up. Positively start your day.

Let's continue on your journey. Along with helping your luck, let's start your lucky quest with a simple exercise. We've all heard of the glass half-full versus half-empty theory. Go to your kitchen cupboard and choose your favorite glass (and yes, we all have that favorite glass.) Squeeze some fresh lemon juice into the glass and fill the glass with warm water. Slowly drink and savor the delicious water. What a lovely, refreshing way to start your lucky day. Did you know there are at least eight benefits to drinking warm lemon water first thing in the morning? Here are some reasons to drink warm lemon water to start your day the lucky lemony way:[1]

- ✓ Boosts your immune system.
- ✓ Flushes toxins.
- ✓ Helps with weight loss.
- ✓ Aids digestion.
- ✓ Is a diuretic.
- ✓ Clears the skin.
- ✓ Freshens breath.
- ✓ Relieves respiratory problems.

What does this have to do with creating luck? It is one of the many steps included in this book to help you design your life, create your luck, and achieve a healthier body and vigorous mind. An empty glass equals a symbol of your former life. As your day progresses, you are going to fill up that glass. This morning, did you wake up to a new day? Lucky you! Some people didn't.

> I love living. I love that I'm alive to love my age. There are many people who went to bed just as I did yesterday evening and didn't wake this morning. I love and feel very blessed that I did.
>
> MAYA ANGELOU

Drop a token in that special glass. Did you have a roof over your head, hot water for your shower, coffee in the pot? Drop, drop, drop those tokens into that glass. Tokens can be whatever you choose and whatever is handy: paperclips, rubber erasers, coins, or marbles. Hmmm, maybe don't use your favorite glass. A sturdy plastic jar might work better. Continue this ritual throughout the day. Your child hugged you, you caught the bus on time, your grumpy co-worker actually smiled at you, your boss complimented you, you forgot your umbrella, and it didn't rain. Oh, look out! That car coming around the corner didn't hit you. By the end of the day your jar will be full. Now you are saying, "Who is this crazy lady? I am not going to walk around all day with a jar." Of course you're not; however, you can keep a little bag in your purse or pocket. Each time you realize you just had a lucky moment, drop in a marble or a small pebble. Alternatively, you can transfer items from one pocket to another (hairbands or colored elastics) from one wrist to another. How many items are in that glass, bag or pocket by the end of the day? I call this luck ritual Jamie's Jar of Gems.

If you are a reader of self-help books or blogs, you will know that this type of idea is not new. But it will serve as a stepping stone to thinking differently about luck.

Since beginning to write this, I have learned that author and innovator, Tim Ferriss, uses a Jar of Awesome to reflect on good things that happen to him. Tim suggests that we need to celebrate the small wins. When something cool happens, you're not going to remember it three months later. Write it down on a slip of paper and drop the paper into your Jar of Awesome. While Tim uses a mason jar, you can use any jar you have available. Reviewing these testimonials can be a type of reverse fortune cookie testimonial that things aren't that bad. This analysis helps you appreciate your small wins and milestones.[2]

> If the grass looks greener on the other side, stop staring. Stop comparing. Stop complaining and start watering the grass you're standing on.
> THE CELTIC CHRISTIAN TRADITION

LUCKY LIST

Before we continue to more concrete ways of increasing your good fortune, let's list some luck. Record five things you want more of in your life. For this exercise, you can't list most people's number one wish; money. Also, none of the items can involve money. Over the next few days and weeks, look for these items in your life. More laughter? More love? More friends? More sleep? More satisfaction at work? More exercise? Keep looking. Keep paying attention. Likely you are already observing more of these special components in your life. Reflect on these occasions. Perhaps you already feel luckier.

DEVELOP AN ATTITUDE OF GRATITUDE
Increase Your Wealth

Do you desire to improve your luck through wealth? Tom Corley[3] is an internationally recognized author who has written extensively on habit and wealth creation. He speaks and writes on success habits of the rich and failure habits of the poor. In his research on gratitude, Mr. Corley found that wealthy, successful people had a happiness habit; a positive mindset. One of the secrets of the wealthy is they practice gratitude.

Appreciate what you have, and in the future, you will likely be better off financially. Grateful people are perceived as more personable and charming; thereby making better managers and often enjoying more success in their careers.[4]

Get Healthier and Happier

People who are unhappy often turn to retail therapy. Those who may be somewhat dejected tend to combat unhappiness by purchasing new things.[5] Individuals who are less materialistic have been found to be happier and more satisfied with life. Concentrate on gratitude rather than buying. Spending less and saving more equals wealth creation.

There are reasons why holidays such as Thanksgiving, Christmas and other non-Christian holidays are so popular. Thinking about all you have boosts your overall sense of well-being; however, don't reserve gratitude for special occasions. Express gratefulness for momentous events such as the birth of a child or completion of a significant project. Appreciation for simple joys is also essential. The greats are grateful every day.

We are fortunate to have much for which to be grateful. Practicing gratitude enhances those riches. Being grateful impacts our mindset and affects our overall level of happiness. These effects tend to be long-lasting.

A review of the research reveals many benefits of gratitude including improved social, emotional and physical well-being:[6]

- » Greater happiness and optimism.
- » Strengthened heart, immune system, and decreased blood pressure.
- » Enhanced feelings of connection in times of loss or crises.
- » Deceased depression, anxiety, and headaches.
- » Better self-care regarding health.
- » Longer and more refreshed sleep.

> Be thankful for what you have; you'll end up having more. If you concentrate on what you don't have, you will never, ever have enough.
> OPRAH WINFREY

The social benefits of an attitude of gratitude make people feel more helpful, convivial and generous. A Berkeley study of one thousand people reported people who practice gratitude feel more forgiving and outgoing. Interestingly, people feel less lonely and less isolated.[7]

Just trying to think of the things for which you feel grateful is enough. This act of thinking of the positive aspects of your life increases serotonin production. Increasing serotonin is what Prozac does.

Having a hard time finding something to appreciate? You can be thankful for this- what matters most is remembering to look in the first place. *"Remembering to be grateful is a form of emotional intelligence."* Expressing gratitude makes your brain happier.[8]

LUCKY LEARNING

STARTING MY LUCKY JOURNEY:

- » Positively begin my day. Every morning when I awake, I look around and count my blessings for three things for which I am thankful.

- » Start my day the lucky lemony way.

- » Use a Jar of Gems or alternative method to record lucky moments.

- » Create a Lucky List of five items I want more of in my life. Observe to see if these items are already in my life.

- » Develop an Attitude of Gratitude.

MY GRATITUDE LIST

1.

2.

3.

4.

5.

CHAPTER 3

IT'S ALL IN THE NAME

> Luck is my middle name.
> Mind you, my first name is Bad.
> TERRY PRATCHETT

What's in a name? You may have the perfect name. You might love your name. If that is the case, don't do a thing with it. Keep it. Praise it. Thank your parents for being wise enough to have bestowed you with such a marvelous moniker. But if you are in the "What the hell were they thinking?" category, here is your chance to become whoever you want to be in the privacy of your living room, even if it's only for a few moments. Become your own Superhero. Who is your favorite? Thor? Wonder Woman? Iron Man? Don a mask. A cape. Jump around your living room. Take a lucky leap. Create your new reality. Believe you are lucky. Have some fun. Be **Super Luck.**

How many of us have ever noticed that the last two letters of the word "name" are "me"? Your name is more important to the luck in your life than you may think. Ever heard of Usain

Bolt? He is the blur of lightning who is currently considered the greatest sprinter of all time. We are not surprised that this bolt of lightning can race down a track like no one else! I have always been fascinated with the connection between names and occupations. When I grew up, the local paper had a bird watcher whose last name happened to be Chickadee. The reporter who wrote the business section had the last name of Cash. And did you know that Buzz Aldrin's mother's maiden name was Moon? Jimmy Kimmel hosted an episode where he spoke with people whose names perfectly match their jobs: volunteer firefighter Les McBurney, dentist Dr. Chip Silvertooth, and contractor Paul Schwinghammer. I once saw a photo of a doctor's name shingle – Dr. B. Gee. Presumably, she is good at helping people stay alive. One person you may not want ever to meet, though, is lawyer Sue Yoo.

An aptronym is a personal name aptly suited to its owner. It turns out there is a name for this phenomenon. It is called nominative determinism-a phenomenon where people seemed to have picked occupations that perfectly suit their name. A Google search of nominative determinism reveals many examples- an architect named Koolhaus, a music teacher named Miss Fiddle who married and became Mrs. Horn, a vicar named Vicker and the biology teacher named Mr. Mould.

NAME YOUR LUCK

> What's in a name? That which we call a rose
> By any other name would smell as sweet.
> **WILLIAM SHAKESPEARE**

(Or Would It?)

Wondering about your name? Jamie Friedlander of success.com suggests that if you're a Jim, Mark, or a Tom, you are lucky. Short, concise names are opportune for men in the workplace. Research gathered by LinkedIn also supports this premise. The top CEO names for men are Jack, Bob, Peter, Bruce, and Fred. However, for women, full names are more common in CEO positions. The top spots are Deborah, Debra, Cynthia, and Carolyn. For women, having a gender-neutral name is a blessing.[1] This is especially true in fields dominated by men, such as technology, banking, law, and engineering.

With what letter does your surname start? Here is where you may have gotten **lucky**. Your last name can hold the key to your success. Throughout school and in any directory or register, names are listed alphabetically. If your initials come earlier in the alphabet, you are more likely to win a Nobel Prize. People with the top names get used to being first. The further down the alphabet your surname comes, the less likely you are to be successful.

Business Insider reported that people with common given names were most likely to be hired. People with names such as Mary, John or James are in luck.[2]

Does all this mean you should change your name? Perhaps, but not likely. However, there are a few strategies you can use to affect your success in the name game.

Business Insider suggests these tips:

Shorten your name or use a nickname. According to a 2011 LinkedIn study of names most associated with the CEO position, most names were short and most-often one syllable names. The same study found that women at the top were more likely to use their full names. The thinking is that men use nicknames to offer a sense of friendliness while women use full names to project professionalism.

Use your middle initial. As reported by the European Journal of Social Psychology, using a middle initial increases people's perception of your intellectual capacity and performance. Middle initial users also had better reviews of their writing quality. Apparently, people also associate a middle initial with a high perceived social status.[3]

> I got my first name from my father, and I got my middle name from someone who obviously didn't think I'd ever run for president.
>
> BARRACK HUSSEIN OBAMA

NAME THAT CHILD

Thinking of calling that new baby boy after Grandpa? You may not want to. It all depends on Grandpa's name.

If you want your son to be a dentist, try naming him Dennis. Or if you want a lawyer in the family, call your daughter 'Laura.' Girls with more feminine names such as Elizabeth (It has several soft consonant sounds.) are more likely to choose the humanities in college. Girls with less feminine sounding names, such as Alex, would take advanced mathematics and science.

A BOY NAMED SUE

This might be a well-known song by Johnny Cash in which, at the end of the song, he declares he would name a son anything but SUE!" Johnny Cash may not have known the science, but he knew the lessons. Beware. Don't create bad luck. Boys with unusual or feminine sounding names can have increased disciplinary problems in middle school.

NAME SIGNALING

Name signaling is what someone's name indicates about their ethnicity, religion, social sphere and socioeconomic background. A child's name may influence how the teacher treats the child, and that treatment, in turn, can affect test scores.

Be aware that your name is just one factor that can affect your luck. Remember, instead of thinking of yourself as Poor Perceval, you can think of yourself as Amazing Amal.

LUCKY LORE

In a 2007 paper, **Moniker Maladies**,[4] Leif Nelson and Joseph Simmons analyzed almost a century of baseball strikeouts. Intriguingly they found that hitters with the initial 'K' had a higher strikeout rate. For non-baseball fans, the letter "K" denotes a strikeout in baseball. Nelson and Simmons also found that graduate students with the initials C and D had a slightly lower grade point average than A and B students. A and B applicants to law school were more likely to go to better colleges.

Are you curious about cruising? Pondering a long sea voyage? Then you may want to think about changing your name. In 1660 when a ship sank off Dover, the only survivor was called Hugh Williams. In 1767 another vessel went down in the same spot, and the sole survivor was called….Hugh Williams. In 1820 a ship capsized on the Thames, and yes, the only man left alive was…Hugh Williams. In 1940 a German mine blew up a boat. There were two lucky survivors, a man and his nephew. They were both named Hugh Williams.[5]

Here are a few fun facts about the name Lucky:

- » Lucky Jackson was the name of Elvis Presley's character in Viva Las Vegas-a very lucky movie for Elvis!
- » Charles Lindbergh was also known as Lucky Lindy.
- » Leif Ericson/Erikson, also known as Leif the Lucky, is thought to be the first European to have arrived in North America (excluding Greenland) before Christopher Columbus.
- » Lucky is a Power Ranger, who has a habit of saying "Yossha lucky!" due to his incredible luck.
- » Lucky is often a nickname for Lucas and its variants.

» In Numerology, people named Lucky have a deep inner desire to express themselves in acting, writing or singing. They yearn to have beauty around them. People with this name tend to have magnetic personalities and be passionate, romantic and compassionate, but may be easily hurt.

LUCKY LEARNING

- » An aptronym is a personal name suited to its owner.
- » Nominative Determinism-people seem to pick occupations suited to their name.
- » For men in the workplace, short, concise names are best.
- » Gender neutral names are advantageous for women.
- » People with common given names are more likely to get hired, with most CEO'S having names that were short, one-syllable names.
- » Women are best to use full names to project professionalism.
- » Using a middle initial increase's people's perception of your intellectual capacity, performance and social status.

Section Two

ATTRACTING LUCK TO YOU

MINDSET AND HABITS

CHAPTER 4

HOW TO MAKE LADY LUCK SMILE UPON YOU - ATTRACTING LUCK TO YOU

> If You're Lucky Enough to be Irish,
> You're Lucky Enough!

Does it seem like fortuitous events always happen to everyone else but you? Do lucky things always happen to "lucky" people? Is the **Luck of the Irish** something you wish you had? Do you desire to have the **Luck Factor?**

> Contrary to what you might think, the phrase "luck of the Irish" didn't originate in the Emerald Isle with leprechauns and rainbows. Historians say the phrase had its roots in the 19th-century America gold rush where many of the notable and successful miners of Irish descent struck it rich in the gold and silver rush.

A LUCKY MINDSET
Traits of the Titans

Now that you have a renewed appreciation for all the luck you have in your life, let's attract more luck. Have you ever asked yourself what successful people do? Are they stronger? Smarter? Think about folks in your community or leaders in your area of expertise. What got them where they are? Are they more deserving than you? What is their lucky secret? They beckon success with a **mastery mindset**. Attracting **luck** into our lives is something we can directly affect and bring forth by embracing and intensifying certain traits. Developing a **Lucky Mindset** enables us to beckon opportunities that can be construed as **lucky**. Roger Clemens once expressed that if you put in the time and have the mindset, will, and desire, anything is possible.

Favored people are luckier than others due to the way they see the world. Lucky people generate their luck through their mindset. Individuals said to have the luck factor create and notice opportunities. Fortuitous people aren't fortunate by accident. They possess traits that make them luckier than others because of the mindset they possess.[1,2]

Cultivating a **Lucky Mindset** requires a collaboration of actions that stimulate the rewards we seek. It is a Mindset in which we believe we can control our destiny. Luck is **desire plus action**. If we are willing and open, we can improve our good fortune. You have every opportunity to create your luck-it is not a paranormal manifestation.

> If you choose not to grow, you're staying in a
> small box with a small mindset.
> People who win go outside of that box.
>
> KEVIN HART

A review of literature and luck reveals much. There is scientific research. There are the habits of the greats, the rich and the brave. And of course, there is also whimsy and folklore.

Is good fortune just a random act of kindness from the universe? Are the life events we consider **'lucky'** really fortuitous? Or are they directly related to the actions we take? Does luck result from a series of actions we conduct on a daily basis?

There is an old joke about luck that goes like so. A guy named Joe constantly finds himself in financial trouble. He is so desperate he decides to ask God for help. "God, please help me. My business is in trouble, and I might lose my house. Please help me win the lottery." Lotto night comes and someone else wins it. Joe again prays, "God, please let me win the lotto!" Lotto night comes and Joe still has no luck. Joe, now despondent, begs God. "God, I don't often ask you for help. I've been a good servant. Please let me win the lotto this one time." Suddenly there is a blinding light. The heavens open. The voice of God booms down, *"Joe, meet me halfway. Buy a ticket."*

Even winning the lottery requires buying a ticket. Our **lucky** life events are linked to our traits, behaviors and activities.

> You could say you are a little lucky. It's not just luck. You still had the idea. You still took action. You still made it happen. Lots of people have ideas. They never do anything with them. You might have some luck too, but you really have positioned yourself well to be lucky.[3]
>
> CHRIS GUILLEBEAU

THE MANY WAYS LUCKY PEOPLE CREATE THEIR LUCK

Lucky, successful people believe you create your luck.

LUCKY PEOPLE FEEL LUCKY

> Luck is Believing You're Lucky
>
> TENNESSEE WILLIAMS

Richard Wiseman who spent fifteen years researching folks' perceptions of luck, and their fate, reported his findings in his book, **The Luck Factor**.[4] Wiseman is a very wise man who reports that the expectations people have, become self-fulfilling prophecies. If you ask a person who is thought to be lucky, why he or she is so lucky, the 'lucky' person is likely to answer that they choose to believe they are lucky. Lucky people believe they are lucky. They know that more often than not, when they accidentally drop a slice of bread slathered in peanut butter, that slice of bread is going to land peanut butter side up. Think positively. Be optimistic.

> May good luck be your friend in whatever you do
> and may trouble always be a stranger to you.
>
> ANONYMOUS

LUCKY PEOPLE BELIEVE IN LUCK

Thomas Corley, in his **Rich Habits**[5] research, reveals that the rich believe in luck. The rich feel they create their own luck.

> Just tell yourself, Duckie,
> you're really quite lucky.
>
> DR. SEUSS

Corley reveals that the rich, through their good habits, good behaviors and confident and controlled emotions, generate their own form of good luck. This is a combination of action and reaction.

For successful people, specific things like habits-good ones in this case-are the cause, and good luck is the effect. Lucky people are persistent in applying good habits. They follow good practices and pursue success for many years.

LUCKY PEOPLE BELIEVE THEY WILL SUCCEED

Since fortunate people think of themselves as lucky; this perpetuates a favorable cycle. This confident belief keeps propitious people striving for what they want and helps them shrug off setbacks. Fortunate people have a sunnier way of thinking. They don't see every misfortune as permanent-it won't last forever.[6]

LUCKY PEOPLE ARE SELF-EMPOWERED

Be a dynamic participant in your life in order to take control of your luck. To live the life you imagine, you must be the one controlling your life. Self-empowered people seek and make their own fortunes by being open to change, being willing to take charge, and perhaps step outside their comfort zones. Titans ask for what they want.

Successful people believe that opportunities stem from their actions and attitude.

Take responsibility for yourself. Lucky people don't wallow in feelings of self-pity and don't believe they are victims of circumstance. People who consider themselves unlucky see life circumstances and luck as something imposed on them; they walk around saying they are so unlucky.

> When you think everything is someone else's fault, you will suffer a lot. When you realize that everything springs only from yourself, you will learn both peace and joy.
>
> — DALAI LAMA

LUCKY PEOPLE ARE OPEN TO NEW OPPORTUNITIES

> Luck is What Happens When
> Preparation Meets Opportunity.
> SENECA

Jeff Goins is a writer who believes we must seek luck-that we can't sit around and wait for opportunities. Luck is often found in hard to reach places that most people are too timid to explore.[7]

Lucky people value fresh experiences. They are open to an intuitive range of possibilities. Fortunate people are receptive to new opportunities. Jayson DeMers[8] in his article 6 *Ways to Actually Increase Your Luck*, asserts that prosperous, lucky people have a *"why not?"* mentality. Jayson, also posits that fortunate people don't sit idly; they find new opportunities by being in motion. When things work out well, the bold decision seems even luckier.

> Fortune favors the bold
> VIRGIL

Richard Branson, founder of the Virgin Group, has been known to say that some of the luckiest people are those willing to take the greatest risks.[9]

Kate Middleton, The Duchess of Cambridge and one of the world's most photographed women, is someone who partially made her luck. In her book, **Kate, The Future Queen**,[10] Katie Nicholl reveals that the Duchess had a last-minute change of heart about school. Kate Middleton had already received her acceptance letter to attend school in Edinburgh when she decided to drop her place, take a gap year and reapply to St. Andrews. Guess who was going to be attending St. Andrews at that time? The palace had announced that Prince William would be attending St. Andrews. Applications shot up by nearly fifty percent. Giving up her place in Edinburgh and reapplying at St. Andrews was a huge risk for Kate Middleton. As we know, the Duchess was accepted, and as they say, the rest is literally "herstory."

The Duchess of Cambridge positively took action to create her own luck. There was a distinct chance that she would not be accepted to St. Andrews. There was an obvious risk that she and the prince would never date, never mind get married. Kate made a **bold** move.

Both in ancient, mystical times and in modern day, stories of elves, shoes for the poor, and good-hearted, generous shoemakers seem to abound. Perhaps as a child growing up you were entertained by the Grimm's Fairy Tale, ***The Elves and the Shoemaker***. In most variations, a poor shoemaker needs money to pay the rent. Being kind and generous, the shoemaker gives away his last pair of shoes to a needy lady. The shoemaker has enough leather to make one more pair of shoes. He cuts out the pieces before going to bed. Elves arrive in the night and make a beautiful pair of shoes which the shoemaker sells for more than the asking price. The shoemaker uses that money to pay the rent, buy food and buy just enough leather to make two more pairs of shoes.

The shoemaker cuts the pieces of leather for two pairs of shoes, and he and his wife go to bed. The mysterious elves come again and make two pairs of beautiful shoes. The shoemaker gives away one pair and sells the other pair to an immensely satisfied customer.

This time the shoemaker buys enough leather for three pairs of shoes and the elves return to make elegant shoes. The shoemaker gives away a set of shoes and sells the two other pairs to happy customers. After a while, the shoemaker and his wife decide to stay up to find out who is making the handsome shoes. They leave a small candle burning and hide behind a curtain. Lo and behold, they are enchanted when they see the elves arrive to sew their shoes. The shoemaker and his wife, wanting to return the kindness of the elves, decide to sew some clothes for the elves, as the elves are naked. The elves are delighted when they put on the clothes. They are freed, never to return.

Perhaps the lesson here is that the shoemaker creates his luck by being kind and generous. Does a benevolent force reward the shoemaker and his wife for their unselfish actions by sending the mysterious elves? Are the magic elves a symbol of the mysteries of the universe? By freeing the elves, does the shoemaker then lose his luck? Perchance the message is the shoemaker has created enough luck that he is now self-sufficient and capable of functioning on his own. The shoemaker has shown determination and persistence. He no longer needs the elves and can set them free.

He Who Does Not Venture Has No Luck.

In his book, **Start Something That Matters**,[11] Blake Mycoskie, the founder of Tom's shoes, recounts the story of how Tom's shoes came to be. While traveling in Argentina, Blake got used to wearing the alpargata, the soft, canvas shoe of the Argentinians; however, many of the children went barefoot as they couldn't afford shoes. Blake met a woman who was collecting shoes and redistributing them. Blake recounts that he thought of starting a shoe-based charity, but soon realized his connections would eventually dry up, and as a result, so would the charity. Blake felt a better solution was to look at what he knew- entrepreneurship and business. Thus, Tom's was born.

A modern-day shoemaker and some elves! Blake is also the creator of the One for One business model- donating a pair of shoes for every pair of shoes sold. (Or perhaps it was really the fairy tale shoemaker?)

Of course, the story is not quite as simple as this. Blake tells of spending days going to country factories in barns to create the prototype of the shoe. In a Tim Ferriss podcast[12], Blake reveals stories of nearly going bankrupt due to various crises. However, he believed in himself and remained steadfast through the hard times, turning his luck around.

The takeaway here is that when the opportunity presented itself, Blake was prepared to grab it and run with it. He also had to take the risk, put in the hard work, the time and the effort. Throughout our lives, many of us have opportunities that we ignore or to which we don't pay attention. We have to be willing to take risks, go outside our comfort zones, work hard and perhaps live uncomfortably for a time.

LUCKY PEOPLE ARE MINDFUL AND PRESENT

Lucky people are alert, with a keen sense of awareness. They pay attention to what is going on around them and to their day-to-day surroundings. They pay attention to their guts, and to their social and emotional intelligence. People considered lucky can often spot a gem of an opportunity. The fortuitous break may present itself, but if we don't act upon it, we won't be any luckier than our unlucky neighbor.

> Life is yin and yang. Hard work and luck work in tandem, not opposite each other. After all, you can get all the lucky breaks in the world, but if you don't take action, they are pretty useless.
>
> KRISTIN WONG [13]

Be aware of opportunities. When fortune seeks you out, be predisposed to accept. There is a psychological term called the **Self Attribution Bias**. Bias is defined as prejudice or a propensity to make decisions while being influenced by an underlying belief. A self-attribution bias is when people attribute favorable outcomes to their skill, but blame unfortunate results on bad luck. The self-attribution bias is due to a tendency to favor explanations that protect our egos. We sometimes overvalue our skills. If things go our way, it is because we did well, we made favorable decisions or beneficial choices. People with a strong, internal locus of control feel they have more control over their destiny. Those with a firm locus of control tend to dismiss luck. Some think if we acknowledge luck, we discredit all our hard work.

There are, however, benefits to acknowledging luck. If you are willing to recognize luck, you are open to finding, recognizing and taking advantage of your good luck. Endorsing your fortunate circumstances can help inspire resourcefulness, as we saw with Blake Mycoskie. The story of Tom's shoes demonstrates elements of all of these features: being mindful and present, recognizing opportunity, being willing to take a risk, being prepared and working hard.

LUCKY PEOPLE ARE PREPARED

The French mathematician, Blaise Pascal, once said,

> Chance favors the prepared mind.

Be prepared. In many ways, anticipation and preparation are the essences of luck. In business and our personal lives, misfortune happens. One never knows how events will turn out. Life isn't planned around a crystal ball. What we do know is that sometimes the ride will be smooth, sometimes exhilarating, often bumpy and occasionally harrowing. We can't determine when and if any of these circumstances will happen. What we can control is whether or not we are prepared for calamity, if it does strike. Those who are ready always fare better than those who aren't prepared. Those who planned are predisposed to luck.

Know the odds! When making a major decision, make sure the odds are in your favor; do as much research as you can for significant decisions. If you don't know what the chances of success are, you are likely to find yourself unlucky if you experience failure. If you know proactively your chances of failure are high, you are unlikely to make that decision.[14]

LUCKY PEOPLE ARE CONSCIENTIOUS

Want a higher income and job satisfaction? Be conscientious. There is a vast amount of research linking conscientiousness with success. Conscientious people are usually reliable, organized and great planners. Conscientious workers set and achieve goals that are consistent with their employer's expectations, so those who are conscientious are very successful.[15]

Conscientiousness was found to be one of the six factors that could be used as an indicator for measuring future leadership potential.

Conscientiousness is a personality trait closely tied to self-control. Self-control predicts success even better than IQ.[16]

Want to live a long, lucky life? Be conscientious. Conscientiousness is the best predictor of a long life.

If you want to be married to the same person for that long life, be conscientious. Conscientiousness is also associated with marital satisfaction.

LUCKY PEOPLE ARE SOCIAL BUTTERFLIES

Do you love to socialize and meet new people? If so, you are in luck. Party on. Make friends. Get social. One predictor of how many "lucky breaks" a person has is how social and interconnected that person is with those around them. This attribute can also relate to taking chances.

In his research, psychologist Richard Wiseman[17] discovered that lucky people interact with a wide-reaching number of people. This increases their odds of chance encounters. Be in the right place at the right time.

Remember that old saying – It's not what you know, but who you know!

Lucky people have a fairly large social group, make friends easily and are involved in their community. Rekindle relationships. Reconnect with people you already know. Go to the dreaded reunions. Try out unique circumstances. Attend events to which you might not normally go. Widen your network. Surround yourself with friends, acquaintances and professional contacts. Do this and feel luckier. It is social karma. In good times, friends may invite you to events, share tickets or introduce you to your future partner or employer. In tough times, those in your large circle provide social-emotional support. You will feel luckier either way.

A CHANCE ENCOUNTER THAT CHANGED THE WORLD

You may be young. You may be old. You may not know a beetle from a cockroach. Or a beetle from a Beatle. But I bet you do know a Beatle from a Bieber. And if you are over a certain age, did you ever wonder how the Beatles met? How did John meet Paul? They first met in Liverpool, on July 6, 1957, when John was fronting the Quarrymen. The Quarrymen's bass player introduced the two. Paul sang some songs by Little Richard and Gene Vincent which the Quarrymen had been struggling to master. Legend has it that Paul and John were both impressed with and admired one another. After some debate, Paul McCartney was invited to join the band. As they say, the rest is history, kicking off the most successful songwriting duo in musical history.

I imagine the conversation went something like this:

"Good Morning. Good Morning. How are you?"

"I Feel Fine."

"I've got a feeling."

"Let's Come together. I Need You."

"Got to get you into my life. Don't let me down. Please Please Me"

"Okay, I Fancy My Chances With You."

The meeting of Paul and John is one chance encounter that musicians, and the world in general, are glad took place. Thankfully, a then fifteen-year-old Paul went out to a garden fete of St. Peter's Church in Woolton, Liverpool, England.

A SERENDIPITOUS NAME

Did you ever wonder how the song name 'Eleanor Rigby came to be? Paul says he chose the title's first name after working with the actress, Eleanor Bron, in the film 'Help.' Paul states that the last name came about one evening as he was walking around Bristol. Paul saw a shop called 'Rigby & Evens Ltd, Wine & Spirits Shippers.' According to Paul, it was a very ordinary name, but exactly what he wanted.[18]

There is, however, a serendipitous twist. In the 1980's, an old gravestone was discovered in St. Peters Parish Church cemetery, in Woolton, Liverpool where Paul and John first met. The name on the stone is Eleanor Rigby.

LUCKY PEOPLE HAVE A DISCOVERY MINDSET

> Two roads diverged in a wood …
> I took the one less travelled by,
> and that has made all the difference.
> ROBERT FROST

When was the last time you made an auspicious discovery or learned something entirely new you weren't expecting, or found money or saw something astonishing? There you were, minding your own business, listening to a podcast while idly strolling along the Riverwalk, reading a book while having a latte macchiato at Starbucks or attending a presentation about a trip you are thinking of taking. It's a sure bet you weren't scurrying through the throngs on the sidewalk trying to make it to work on time by covering nine minutes' worth of foot-travel in three minutes so you wouldn't be late for work. Or watching the latest episode of your favorite show on Netflix. Wise Ol' Google tells us that something serendipitous occurs or is discovered by chance in a happy or beneficial way.

Isn't finding that money, learning that surprising fact about a destination you are planning to visit or observing the wingspan of a bald eagle the best kind of discovery!

Fortuitous discoveries will only be found if we pursue incidental encounters; if we expand our boundaries. We need to be open. We need to explore. We need chance encounters with the world outside our neighborhood, outside our experience base. We learn and discover through serendipitous engagements with an array of people from all communities, cultures and countries.

We can increase our luck by embracing random encounters. By being aware and insightful, we expand our opportunities to make meaningful connections with the larger world. Adopting a discovery mindset moves us beyond our narrow and perhaps stifling mini-world. We look upon people who travel, who seek out new ventures, who build successful businesses, who create something new and we admire them and call them lucky.

They say every journey begins with a first step. If you are stuck on repeat day after day, you will have the same results day after day. If you live in a large city, visit an area of the municipality you don't frequent regularly. Try taking a different route to work. Join a state of the art group or an association you may not usually seek out. Investigate learning a new skill. If you can, you should travel as much as possible. Venture to new countries. If you don't have the time or the budget, try sightseeing in a new city or town in your own country. Wander into quaint little shops. Visit independent bookstores. Drop into mom and pop businesses. You may chance upon new friends, a special friend, or encounter unanticipated work opportunities.

A discovery mindset means moving away from fear. We often change our minds about things; therefore, we can change our fear mindset. The more unique actions we undertake, the more likely lucky things will happen.

LUCKY BIRDS OF A FEATHER FLOCK TOGETHER: DON'T LET YOUR GAGGLE DRAG YOU DOWN

Like attracts like. Winners are attracted to winners and whiners are attracted to whiners. We unknowingly seek out others with whom we feel comfortable. The people with whom we associate likely have a similar work ethic, kindred traits, and comparable habits, as well as complementary outlooks. Sound familiar? Increase your exposure to people you consider fortunate and expand your circle of success. While you are out there being a social butterfly you can boost your chances of becoming lucky, accomplished, rich and happy by associating with other lucky, notable or outstanding folk. Cultivate an orchard of people you view as winners. Plant seeds of positivity along with them. The seeds will become trees. The trees will burst into glorious blossoms. Your luck will be in full bloom. The blossoms will further become fruit. Sow and watch your luck grow.

Don't aimlessly formulate relationships with others who impede you. Build your nest in a garden of positives. Fly with a flock that lifts you up.

LUCKY PEOPLE DO LIKE THE COWBOYS AND 'PARTNER UP': FIND A MENTOR

> If I have seen further than others,
> it is by standing on the shoulders of giants.
> **SIR ISAAC NEWTON**

Still waiting for luck to find you, particularly at work or in your new entrepreneurial adventure? Seek wisdom. Reach out your hand to Lady Luck. Find a mentor, or two or three. Way back in the day, mentoring was the favored way. In the ancient times of our forefathers, it was how everyone learned their craft. Your craft was your business: ironworking, horseshoeing, baking, dressmaking. One became an apprentice and learned from the master, presumably a parent, other relative or friend. In today's world, it is likely you are working for and with strangers. Perhaps you are an entrepreneur starting a business alone. There are many reasons why you need a mentor. At the very minimum, mentors provide information and knowledge; yet, a mentor is so much more. A mentor inspires, connects, stretches, and helps steep you in the knowledge of those from whom you aspire to learn. Don't assume you have to create your luck alone. Others can be a great support as you strive to improve in life, seek your fortune or aim to master a goal at work. There is a reason country singers move to Nashville and artists and writers move to Paris. Bill Gates often referred to Warren Buffet as his mentor. Steve Jobs mentored Mark Zuckerberg.

> Tell me and I forget, teach me and I may remember, involve me and I learn.
> BENJAMIN FRANKLIN

Mentors find ways to stimulate personal and professional growth. According to an article published by the University of Cambridge,[19] research has found the most effective people have different mentors for the diverse areas of their personal and professional lives. The key is clarity. You must identify why you are seeking a mentor. You need to ask yourself some pertinent questions. "What do I want to learn?" "What do I want to know about that?" "Who do I know that can teach me that?" What is your greater goal? What impact do you want to have on the world? What is your greater vision? Your mentor will then be someone who has the knowledge you are seeking to gain, and who is willing to take the time and make an effort to share that knowledge.

Perhaps you are a young millennial seeking luck at work. Invite possible mentors for coffee or lunch. Establish positive, authentic relationships. In the world of millennials, your job may not be there in five years, but the people will be.

Keep in touch with the people whom you genuinely admire. Share engaging information, ask for advice, and follow up. Be sure to listen and pay attention. Ask interesting questions. Show gratitude. Thank your mentor.

Reciprocate whenever possible. You know more than you think you do and you have different strengths. If you are younger, it is quite likely you are more social media savvy or more aware of new, useful apps than a more seasoned co-worker.[20]

In the serendipitous way of the world, the circle of knowledge comes around. Once more we see the lucky mindset traits: taking responsibility for oneself, asking for what we want, being social and being prepared.

SIX DEGREES OF KEVIN BACON: LUCKY PEOPLE BUILD A NETWORK

Along with a well-founded relationship with a mentor or mentors, connect with disparate groups of people to build a network. As noted earlier, lucky people consider themselves lucky. Studies show if you associate with people who consider themselves lucky, your luck will improve.

Often, opportunities made available due to friend-of-friend connections appear to be lucky. They are also the result of good networking. Lucky people create their luck by associating with people who consider themselves lucky.[21] Create a network of people who represent a varied range of fields.

A good network delivers access to diverse skill sets and power. When it comes to networking, you might think it luckier to have more friends than acquaintances, but this is not so. The research tells us otherwise. When seeking a job, most of us approach our closest, strong ties such as family members, friends, and colleagues. However, as luck would have it, it would be to your advantage to play the *'Six Degrees of Kevin Bacon'* game. Sociologist Mark Granovetter demonstrated that people were 58 percent more likely to get a job through their weak ties than their strong ties.[22] Our strong ties-family and friends-all know the same circle of people, contacts, and information. Our weak ties travel in different spheres and reach diverse networks.

One such way to meet people with whom to network is through shared activities but not direct work activities. Look to sports teams, community service ventures, and volunteer work.

LUCKY PEOPLE ARE HAPPY

Clap along with this one, but what I'm about to say is not crazy. Many of us go through life thinking we will be happy once we get that promotion, lose ten pounds, go on a nice vacation, or attain our goals. We believe if we achieve success, we will be happier. Wrong. Research shows that isn't true. Shawn Achor is the best-selling author of *The Happiness Advantage*.[23] For years he studied happiness and found that happiness brings success. Mr. Achor's research showed that once people achieve a goal, they are briefly happier, but then they are off searching for the next thing. Shawn suggests flipping the formula. Focus on increasing happiness and you end up increasing success.

Optimistic people are more successful than pessimistic people. If you want to increase success at work and be more compelling, be happy. According to an article reported in the Huffington Post, happy people were more productive.[24] People who are happy at work are more motivated and more committed.

LUCKY LEARNING

- We can attract more luck into our lives with a lucky mindset.
- Luck is desire plus action.
- Lucky people feel lucky. Luck is believing you are lucky.
- Rich people believe in luck and generate their own success through their habits, behaviors and positive, controlled emotions.
- Good habits are the cause, and good luck is the effect.
- Lucky people are self-empowered.
- Lucky people are open to new opportunities and value a range of possibilities.
- Lucky people take risks and go outside their comfort zones.
- Lucky people are mindful and present; noticing and acting upon fortuitous opportunities.
- Due to the Self-Attribution Bias, we attribute positive outcomes to our skill but blame unfortunate results on bad luck.
- By acknowledging luck, we are open to finding, recognizing and taking advantage of our good luck. Chance favors the prepared mind.
- Lucky people are conscientious.
- Lucky people are social.

- Winners attract winners. Seek out other lucky people.
- Lucky people value mentors and build a diverse network.
- Lucky people are happy.

MY LUCKY MINDSET ACTIONS

1.

2.

3.

4.

5.

CHAPTER 5

LUCKY HABITS

> Winning is a Habit
>
> VINCE LOMBARDI

Vince Lombardi, considered by some to be the greatest football coach in NFL history and credited with turning the Green Bay Packers into one of the stars of the NFL, once said that winning was something you did all the time, not just once in a while.

Who doesn't like to win! Let's invest in winning.

Here is why.

Thomas Corley is the author of **Rich Habits: The Daily Success Habits of Wealthy Individuals**.[1] According to an article in Business Insider, Mr. Corley found that rich people think differently. Rich people believe their habits have a significant impact on their lives.

Wealthy people think bad habits create detrimental luck and good habits create "opportunity luck," meaning they create the opportunities for people to make their own luck.

Our daily habits, as dull as they may be, are the secret to success, failure, or mediocrity. Our habitual behaviors, both physical and mental, and the choices we make, are the cause of wealth and poverty.

Studies on habits show that 40 percent of all our activities, both physical and mental, are habits.[2]

Have you tried to start a new lucky habit but not been able to? Do I hear the moans and groans of past resolutions reverberating off the gym walls? Did you maybe make it until 5 o'clock January 1st until you had that first beer, a glass of wine or cigarette? Did it seem like all your efforts were hijacked? You can stop feeling guilty. It's not your fault. There is some science behind the fact that it's hard for us to start a new productive habit or ditch a bad practice.

Habits are the human version of Google. They have a purpose, which is to save us work. Patterns allow us to quickly perform tasks. Habits help us conserve brain fuel. When Google recognizes that you often go to a particular site or notices your favorites, it profiles you. It saves you steps by analyzing your searches. The mind does something similar. When the brain sees cells frequently communicating, it instructs the cells to begin a habit. Just as Google saves us from work, habits protect the mind from work. Therefore, the brain uses less fuel, which is glucose.

It's all about that dreaded glucose. While it provides us with energy, it is also like a Brobdingnagian spider that has taken over our body, preventing us from creating the good habits we desire to instill in our life. Glucose keeps us stuck in a web even as we try to escape the bondage of those silken strands and form new habits that are good for us. To counter the **Evil Force of Bad Habits** you need to don your super-hero mask and cape from Chapter 3 or become your version of Spidey-Man to break through that tensile habit-busting spider silk.

Just as there is science behind why it is hard to break a bad habit, thankfully there is also science behind how to create a good habit. First, let's take a quick look at how habits become habits.

According to Margaret Thatcher, former Prime Minister of the United Kingdom, we should be careful about our thoughts since they become words. Words can become actions which may become habits. Habits can become character, which ultimately becomes our destiny.

> What we think we become.

YOU'VE BEEN TRIGGERED, GOTTEN LOOPY AND BEEN REWARDED - ALL AT THE SAME TIME!

The brain searches for triggers in the environment to pair with a habit. This combination allows the brain to work less, causing you to engage in the habit unconsciously. These are the most common triggers.

Visual Triggers

Have you ever thought about why your stomach rumbles when you see the Golden Arches? Perhaps when you are shopping you suddenly have a desire to buy a candy bar you don't need or a five-dollar coffee at Starbucks.

Auditory Signals

Does the fizzing sound of a beer or soda being popped open immediately make you want one? Have you ever been in a public place and a ringtone or an email alert makes everyone check their phones? These are specific auditory triggers. Chances are you use some on a regular basis. Your morning alarm, for example.

Time Triggers

Most of us mindlessly get up in the morning, wander into the bathroom, brush our teeth, shower, make coffee, and eat breakfast. Time is the trigger here. We don't even think about these early morning habits. Later in the day, the clock tells us it is time for a regularly scheduled meeting or lunch. Or hooray, it is time to go home. Nighttime can trigger T.V. watching, wine drinking, exercising or working on a hobby.

Association Triggers

People with whom we associate can trigger a behavior. The elicited action could be a positive behavior such as going to a gym, or perhaps a harmful activity such as dining out on junk food.

Once the behavior is triggered and you have acted on the trigger, you are rewarded. You drink the coffee, eat the chocolate, go home from work and watch T.V. You have now completed a loop: a trigger, a routine or habit and a reward.

TYPES OF HABITS

There are two types of habits:

1. Ordinary habits
2. Keystone habits

Ordinary Habits are the simple, essential habits of your everyday life: which shoe you put on first, your morning routine: the order in which you shower, brush your teeth, etc., what chair you sit in to eat a meal, which shoe you tie first, or what side of the bed you sleep on.

Keystone Habits:

Merriam-Webster defines a keystone as follows:

» The wedge-shaped piece at the crown of an arch that locks the other pieces in place

» Something on which associated things depend for support

Keystone habits, a term coined by Charles Duhigg,[3] are the essential practices to establish. The central piece that leads to the development of multiple good habits is a keystone habit. Keystone habits help lock the other habits in place. Keystone habits are the start of a chain effect. The significance of keystone habits is that you only need to change a few practices to have a ripple effect on your outcomes. Here are two diverse but effective examples. One monumental keystone habit is developing a daily routine. Charles Duhigg, the author of *The Power of Habit*[4], writes that daily consistency impacts our health, financial security, productivity and very importantly, our happiness. Do you want children who achieve higher grades and have greater emotional control? Start the keystone habit of having family dinners.

DO YOU OWN YOUR HABITS OR DO THEY OWN YOU?

Reinvigorate your lucky habits. Use your newfound knowledge of keystones and triggers to create, model and reinforce habits similar to those of successful people.

GET TRIGGER HAPPY

First, a quick reminder that Habits are the small decisions we make and the actions we perform every day, accounting for about 40 percent of our day. Somewhat of a formidable number, isn't it? It doesn't have to be as, luckily, there is research to help us.

Let's start with the dreaded diet word. Many people (okay almost all of us) want to lose weight. Before I knew about the habit of habits, I lost weight using a well-known weight loss point system. Interestingly, I used triggers without realizing how important they are. For me, the diet journey started when I saw a photograph of myself and had one of those, "Oh, my, who is that big fat blob?" moments. I then printed the photo and stuck it on my fridge. After that, every time I went to the refrigerator to scope out ice cream or other goodies, I saw that blob. I was triggered to not eat the junk food. Once I realized that system was working somewhat well, (the salted caramel ice-cream was sooo good) I added a photo of a gorgeous work-out model to the pantry door (okay, I know, but hope does spring eternal). In this case I was triggered to go for a workout. I was using a visual trigger to remove a poor habit of eating too much ice-cream while using another trigger to start a positive habit of exercising. The weight loss habit became a keystone habit. It led to breakthroughs in other areas such as exercising, healthy eating, and more productive lifestyle changes.

You, too, can use triggers to start your good habits. Remember, triggers can be visual, as in my case, but they can also be auditory, associative or time cues. Sometimes you can combine more than one trigger. Let's say you've decided to start a walking habit. Why not invite a friend to join you (associative). Perhaps you plan to go for your walk every Tuesday evening at 7:00 (time). You can get proactive about setting this habit and program a timer with an audible reminder. In this case, a walking habit may become a keystone habit in the reverse order of the above weight loss habit: walking, weight loss, healthy eating. A healthier lifestyle in general.

Let's not forget that we need a reward to help establish the habit. And no, it doesn't have to be the salted caramel ice-cream. You and your friend could go for a relaxing massage, a cup of tea or simply go home for a warm bath or to watch some sports. Have you been trying to convince your spouse or partner that you need a new tech toy? Fitness trackers reinforce, motivate and reward by turning exercise into a type of game that provides almost instant reinforcement.

I realize that getting skinny and healthy isn't necessarily going to get you lucky, successful and prosperous (although it might). So, let's find out what the lucky habits are.

LUCKY LEARNING

- » Daily Habits represent at least 40 percent of all our day-to-day activities.

- » Ordinary habits are easier to adopt and stand on their own.

- » **Keystone** habits are unique because they affect other patterns. Keystone habits are the most potent habits, harder to instill and harder to eliminate.

- » Without our being aware of it, habits impact our lives in many ways. They are the cause of positive or unhealthy relationships, good and bad health, happiness and sadness, wealth and poverty.

- » **Lucky,** prosperous people have more rich habits than poor habits.

- » Poor people have more harmful habits than rich habits.

CHAPTER 6

DISCOVERING THE LUCKY HABITS

> You will never plough a field
> if you only turn it over in your mind.
>
> Irish Proverb

Good daily habits are the foundation of success. Successful people differ from unsuccessful people in their daily practices. Successful people have many good daily habits and only a few bad ones.

Have you ever asked yourself why the fortunate few-or many- have what they have? Why them and not you? Or for that matter, who are the fortunate few? For most of us the answer is varied. What makes successful people the way they are? How did the world-class performers get to where they are? Yes, this book is about luck and some people are born under a lucky star or under that fourth leaf of a four-leaf clover. Some of the lucky-born continue to thrive. Others don't. What makes the difference?

How are some people able to rise from the ashes to become a phoenix? Hard work and diligence certainly come into play. But, you say, I work hard too. Yes, yes, you do. Read on to see what else you can undertake. What is it that world-class performers do? What do they have in common?

THE HABITS OF SUCCESSFUL PEOPLE: LUCKY PEOPLE MODEL SUCCESSFUL PEOPLE

> Early to bed and early to rise, makes a man healthy, wealthy, and wise.
>
> BENJAMIN FRANKLIN

THE EARLY BIRD GETS THE WORM

While Dolly Parton loved to sing about 9 to 5, working those hours isn't likely what made her successful. The early bird wins. It seems we must rise early. Whatever happened to the night owl?

According to an article in the huffingtonpost.com[1], "Ninety percent of executives wake up before 6 a.m. on weekdays and nearly 50 percent of self-made millionaires wake up at least three hours before their workday actually begins."

The extra hours help provide a belief that we have control over our lives. It gives us a sense of confidence-that extra time to deal with unexpected events.

In an interview with CNBC MAKE IT,[2] Shark Barbara Corcoran revealed that she tries to make the most of every minute of every day. For Corcoran, the morning is especially important because it is her most productive time. Corcoran prioritizes her tasks as A, B or C. A tasks, the tasks where the gold is, are always scheduled in the morning. Barbara also notes that, luckily, time is fair; we all have the same twenty-four hours in a day. It is how we use our twenty-four hours that counts.

The habit of waking up early has numerous benefits. It helps ensure you will get to work or school on time. By leaving earlier, you can avoid the "bad luck" of getting stuck in traffic. Second, you will be far less rushed. Being rushed and stressed creates unnecessary anxiety and pressure, which are not only bad for your health, they can cause unneeded gaffes and blunders. Arising early may have you at your desk before your boss, earning you extra kudos along with some well-earned "**luck**" when it is time for that next raise.

Want to Know What Some Other Self-Made Millionaires do Before Breakfast?

» Make-Up Millionaire/Vlogger/Entrepreneur Michelle Phan does serious morning multi-tasking: squats while brushing her teeth; reading emails while doing push-ups.

» Shark Daymond John reviews his list of seven goals.

» Twitter co-founder CEO Jack Dorsey mediates for thirty minutes, then goes for a six-mile run.

Go. Be a Shark!

WATCH YOUR WAISTLINE

Rich people watch their waistlines by counting calories and exercising every single day.

Aerobic exercise has a whole range of benefits, including improving memory and thinking skills. A review of exercise and the aging process shows that working out can slow down the aging process and shave off almost a decade from one's biological age. The important concept here, though, is vigorous exercise.

Time to get moving! Go for a jog. Jump on that elliptical machine or treadmill. If the word treadmill has always meant "dreadmill" to you, pair using the treadmill with an activity you enjoy such as watching T.V. or listening. As noted above, through the use of audiobooks, you can pair exercise with listening to books. For people who find exercise boring, this is a wonderful way to be entertained while walking or using the treadmill. You can also hold meetings via Skype or FaceTime or dictate notes for your morning meeting.

EXERCISE EARLY

> I have to exercise in the morning before my brain figures out what I'm doing.
> MARSHA DOBLE

Sorry, night owls, the lucky rich and successful do seem to get up early! Two benefits of morning exercise are stress reduction and fighting depression. Richard Branson, the billionaire founder of Virgin Group, has been known to say he rises every day around 5 a.m. to exercise. We can't deny he is one lucky guy! Mark Zuckerberg also rises and exercises early.

> I make sure I work out at least three times a week — usually first thing when I wake up.
>
> MARK ZUCKERBERG

While you are up and at it, ensure that some of that exercise is weight training. Weight training can help prevent cognitive decline. Resistance training has been shown to improve several aspects of cognition, particularly in older adults-notably in memory and memory-related tasks. Improved executive functioning is one of the major benefits of resistance training. Executive functioning is the brain command center that organizes all the tasks in a person's life such as planning, researching, and organizing. If you want to be an executive, get into weight lifting! [3]

If you can't exercise early, be sure you do exercise, particularly if you want to join the 'lucky long lifers club.' Time clicks away for us all. Exercise can extend a life-span by up to five years. Working out slows aging at the cellular level. Whatever physical training and motivators you choose, commit to establishing exercise as a habit, almost like taking a prescription medication. After all, they say that exercise is medicine, and that can go on the top of anyone's list of reasons to work out. [4]

MEDITATE

If getting up early to exercise sounds too much like heavy lifting for so early in the morning, other very successful people wake up at 5 a.m. to meditate. Meditation helps clear our minds so we can focus on the day ahead instead of getting overwhelmed with everything happening around us. Meditation helps lower heart rate and decreases blood pressure, even when the person is not meditating. When you are less stressed and relaxed, you are more open and more likely to notice those chance opportunities and act upon them. You may be additionally willing to socialize and network.

Other benefits of meditation include:[5]

- » Enhanced creativity.
- » Sharper focus.
- » Increased memory.
- » Improved concentration.
- » Expanded self-awareness.
- » Slowed aging.
- » Increased happiness.
- » Benefits cardiovascular and immune health.
- » Helps prevent emotional eating and smoking.
- » Assists with better decision making and problem-solving.
- » Longevity * I consider living longer really lucky!

Super-achievers who reportedly meditate include Oprah, Arianna Huffington, and Jerry Seinfeld. When Tim Ferriss sat down with more than 200 executives, leaders, and other people at the heights of their fields for his new book, *Tools of Titans*, he found that 80 percent had "some form of guided mindfulness practice." [6]

Meditation may be a habit that forms a foundation for other best practices. Leo Babauta of zenhabits.net[7] says that meditating is the most important habit he has formed. It is the habit that helped him establish all his other habits. For Leo, meditation is a keystone habit. Perhaps because meditation is correlated with increased goal-setting. (Duhigg.)

READ BOOKS LIKE THIS ONE!

World class performers read non-fiction every day. When they do read, they read for self-improvement. President Harry Truman once said, **"Not all readers are leaders, but all leaders are readers."** The Business Insider[8] reports that Bill Gates reads close to fifty non-fiction books per year. Elon Musk, the CEO of Tesla, credits a love of books for his vast knowledge of rockets. Mark Cuban, the self-made billionaire and a well-known Shark, spends three hours reading almost every day. He does this to keep an advantage in his field. Cuban says that billionaires are constant learners. Oprah Winfrey, a well-known avid reader, started her famous book club. Reading for learning is a natural habit for associating with triggers. When you get into your car or onto the subway to go to work, you can listen to an audiobook. You can also pair walking or a treadmill workout with listening to an audiobook. Replace the T.V./treadmill habit with an audiobook-treadmill routine. This pairing is especially productive if your life is hectic.

Here is another lucky benefit of book reading. If you read books more than 3.5 hours per week, you can increase your lifespan by almost two years. The same study by Yale University also found that people who read books showed stronger cognitive abilities such as recall and counting backward.[9] Reading books creates cognitive engagement which improves vocabulary, thinking skills and concentration. Book reading affects empathy, social perception, and emotional intelligence. These results all help us live longer. Reading newspapers and magazines does not have the same effect unless one reads them more than seven hours per week.[10]

Reading has been shown to prevent stress, dementia, and depression while enhancing confidence, decision-making, and overall life satisfaction.

Wealthy people are more likely to read than those who make a lower income. The Huffington Post writes that one habit ultra-successful people have in common is that they read.[11] A lot. The Pew Research Center states that adults with an annual household income of less than $30,000 are about twice as likely as the most affluent adults to be non-book readers.[12]

> The more you read,
> the more things you will know.
> The more that you learn,
> the more places you'll go.
>
> DR. SEUSS

ENGAGE IN NEW ACTIVITIES

There are fascinating, fun ways to participate in novel activities:

1. Expand your vocabulary or learn a new language.

2. Dance like nobody's watching. If you are not a gym-rat, you could choose to dance as your form of exercise, and with good reason. Dancing is helpful for your brain as it is a decision-making process. Freestyle dancing is especially beneficial. Dancing increases neural activity by forcing you to integrate several brain activities at once: kinesthetic, rational, musical and emotional.

3. Learn an instrument or create artwork. Both of these stimulating activities promote new neural networks and encourage better brain connectivity.

4. Try mini-brain challenges such as brushing your teeth with your non-dominant hand, eat bites of dinner with your eyes closed or take a different route to work or the store.

5. Learn tai chi, which has been shown to boost thinking skills.

LISTEN TO YOUR MOTHER - MAKE YOUR BED

Making one's bed has become the heavyweight of habits. In a commencement speech given at the University of Texas, U.S. Navy Admiral William H. McCraven[13] noted that if we make our bed every morning we will have accomplished the first task of the day. Admiral McCraven remarked that achieving this minor task instills us with a small sense of pride, which encourages us to carry out and complete another task.

Making your bed is one of Charles Duhigg's keystone habits.[14] Duhigg correlates making your bed with better productivity, greater success at sticking with a budget and a stronger sense of well-being.

According to the author of *The Happiness Project*, Gretchen Rubin, making one's bed is the number one way to elicit impactful change.[15]

PAY YOURSELF FIRST

Lucky, successful people are in the habit of paying themselves first. This custom does not mean spending money on yourself! It means setting aside a certain portion of your income the day you get paid before you spend any discretionary money. Move yourself to the front of the line. Saving or investing for the future is a powerful habit to develop. I can hear many of you yelling at this book, "But I don't have any extra money to invest!" Remember some of our superstars? Oprah, Jim, Shania? Did they have extra money to invest at the beginning? Like many of the other positive habits we want to start, perhaps we need to start small. Speak to your employer about having an extra two, twenty, fifty or one hundred dollars automatically deducted from your paycheck and invested for you. You can also automate the transaction through your bank. As time goes on and you find you can easily get by without that money, you can gradually increase the amount you save.

Challenge yourself to save by **not** spending. Choose not to have that five-dollar designer coffee. Instead, pair that urge with a walk to the bank and deposit that money immediately. You have not only invested five-dollars, you've also invested in your health. Make **Lucky Lattes**. You can peruse the internet to find delicious coffee recipes that don't require fancy ingredients or an expensive machine. Use a travel mug to take your coffee with you. An added benefit is lower blood pressure from not having to wait in a long line up to order your coffee and risk being late for work. Shark Kevin O'Leary (with a good, lucky, Irish name) says he refuses to fork over his hard-earned dollars to coffee shops. *"Do I pay two dollars and fifty cents for a coffee? Never, never, never do I do that,"* O'Leary tells CNBC Make It. *"That is such a waste of money for something that costs twenty cents. I never buy a frappe-latte-blah-blah-blah-woof-woof-woof for two dollars and fifty cents."* [16]

Look for other small ways to save money. Unless you need to entertain clients over lunchtime, brown bag your lunch. Not only will you reduce your spending, but you will also reduce your waistline. Invest in a good quality, reusable water bottle and save money by not buying water or other drinks on a daily basis. You are committing not only to your health, but also to the environment and saving money!

TAKE NOTE

Write it down. Jot down notes and reminders the old-fashioned way or use an app on your phone. But don't forget to do it or you'll forget what it is you want to remember. According to social-economist Randall Bell, Ph.D.,[17] successful people plan out their day and write things down. Take note. Millionaires are 289 percent more likely to maintain a calendar and a to-do-list than those who are less financially successful. Bell cites both Bill Gates and Richard Branson are devoted note takers.

Richard Branson has observed that if he hadn't taken notes, many of Virgin's companies would not exist. Studies show that the actual process of taking notes, type-written or longhand, helps people enhance their learning and achieve their goals. If you want to achieve your aims, write down your intentions and share them. Researchers at the Dominican University of California estimated that a person's chances of success increased by 33 percent when they completed this process.[18]

> When inspiration calls, you've got to capture it.
> RICHARD BRANSON

JOURNAL

> In my life, writing has been an important exercise to clarify what I believe, what I see, what I care about, what my deepest values are. The process of converting a jumble of thoughts into coherent sentences makes you ask tougher questions.
> BARACK OBAMA

Do you love to write? Do you love the sweet smell of newly printed paper, the feel of a new pen? You are in luck. Use your love of writing to keep a journal. The simple act of writing a few sentences or paragraphs can have a profound effect on your life for the better.

Do you hate to write but have a phone? Lucky you. Like to walk? Walk and talk. Record your daily journal sentences.

Have a busy, busy life but a long commute? Use this time to write or record journal entries. But, you say, my life is busy, busy and this is my relax time. Why should I journal?

Studies have shown there are many surprising benefits to keeping a journal. You can profit from journaling, all the while strengthening your lucky life.

You may get more intelligent. Do you like to be on the cutting edge? It is a hot topic, but there is some research that journaling may increase intelligence. And who doesn't want to get smarter? An article in the Huff Post[19] notes the University of Victoria has suggested that writing and language learning have a positive correlation with intelligence. Do you want to understand your partner, children or co-workers better? Journaling may also help increase your emotional intelligence. Emotional intelligence is your ability to recognize and discern your feelings and other people's emotions and like them appropriately. This skill helps guide thinking and behavior, adapt to environments and achieve one's goals.

Do you have serendipitous moments in your life? Would you realize it if you did or would you be too busy working, parenting, stressing, complaining about the life you want to change to pay attention? Lucky opportunities are available to us, but we need to pay attention to them to take advantage of the opportunities they provide.

Richard Wiseman, author of **The Luck Factor**,[20] conducted a study in which participants were instructed to keep a luck journal and told to write down everything lucky that happened to them. The participants started paying attention to events that went their way and began interpreting the events as lucky. They began believing in luck and feeling lucky. Paying attention to serendipitous moments or opportunities allows us to take advantage of these possibilities that may otherwise be lost. We might let them go by unnoticed and later feel unlucky when we realize we didn't act upon an opportunity.

Writing down fortuitous events into a journal is literally a ***stroke of luck***.

Recognizing our luck by writing in a gratitude journal may increase our good fortune. A group of researchers at the University of Miami conducted an intriguing piece of research consisting of three groups writing in diaries; however, what the three groups wrote in the diaries was entirely different. The first group wrote about things that had made them feel grateful; the second group noted things that had made them feel irritated and the third group simply recorded events. After ten weeks, the researchers found quite striking changes in the group which had recorded feelings of gratitude. These changes included less frequent and less severe aches and pains and improved sleep quality. The participants reported greater happiness and alertness and, quite interestingly, they described themselves as more outgoing and compassionate. They also expressed feeling less likely to feel lonely and isolated. The other groups did not report these changes and no similar changes were observed in the second and third groups. Other noted benefits of journaling include reduced anxiety and diminished aggressive impulses.[21]

We have fortuitous moments every day, and we often have lucky coincidences. Don't let these serendipitous moments pass you by without notice. Create a coincidence journal to record your fortunate occasions. Document when good stuff shows up. Reflect on the coincidence. Did you happen to run into someone about whom you were thinking? Did you find the object for which you were looking? Did you discover the piece of information you needed? Optimists and happy people tend to notice opportunities and take advantage of them. Research on optimists and happy people shows that they tend to enjoy more success and satisfaction in life.

In an article discussing how to use a coincidence journal, author Elizabeth Scott[22] writes that optimists notice lucky coincidences. Positive thinkers see the potential that fortuitous happenings bring. As you reflect on your journal entries, you may notice these opportunities and be ready to act upon them.

Journaling can also bring you luck at work. Keeping a written record can come in handy when reflecting on career goals. Pick up your work diary and look back over the things you did well. This contemplation may help you have more luck with your future career goals. You may be able to pick out a pattern of things you want to follow, career-wise. Your achievements and awesome moments not only boost your self-esteem, but they also give you great justification for a raise or promotion during a work review.[23]

Regular writing in a journal forces you to be aware of your actions and behaviors. If you're looking to watch what you eat—keeping a food diary is a great way to start paying closer attention. It is one way that's been proven to help people eat more healthfully. Similarly, just writing down positive things that happened to you or tracking your mood can help you identify favorable patterns in your life that are repeatable, and that you should make time for—not to mention things that make you feel bad or throw you off your game that should be eliminated.

Scientific evidence supports that journaling provides other unexpected benefits. The act of writing accesses your left brain, which is analytical and rational. Occupying your left brain, frees your right brain to create, intuit and feel. In sum, writing removes mental blocks and allows you to use all of your brainpower to better understand yourself, others and the world around you. Begin journaling and begin experiencing these benefits.[24]

A GRATITUDE JOURNAL

Keeping a gratitude journal helps lower stress levels and helps you feel calm at night. A gratitude journal can help you gain perspective on what you truly appreciate in life and help you focus on what matters. This focal point may help you eliminate things from your life that you do not value or which are harmful or unlucky. A gratitude journal can help you become more self-aware so you can appreciate all the luck in your life.

VOLUNTEER

> Volunteer to see how lucky you are. Create luck for others.
>
> MARGARET THATCHER

According to Tom Corley of 16 Rich Habits,[25] nearly three-quarters of rich people volunteer a minimum of five hours a month. For those who struggle financially, only one in ten does this.

If you recall, one way of attracting luck to you is by getting social. What better way to do this than by volunteering, and coincidentally, networking! Often nonprofits and boards are made up of wealthy, successful people.

> If you think you are too small to be effective, you have never been in bed with a mosquito.
> BETTY REESE

Those who volunteer, do so for a variety of reasons. Most often it is to give back to our community. Sometimes we end up volunteering for a particular organization that provided support for ourselves or a loved one. We may decide to support a cause about which we are passionate. Some of us volunteer through our church. Our volunteer efforts might take place just a few blocks from home, or we might find ourselves half-way across the world eating strange foods and hearing a unique language. We volunteer because it makes a difference, but the most significant difference may be in us! Take steps toward your destiny. Count your lucky blessings while others are counting their misfortunes.

> People are lucky and unlucky not according to what they get absolutely, but according to the ratio between what they get and what they have been led to expect.
> SAMUEL BUTLER

Helping others kindles happiness, as many studies have demonstrated. When Social Science and Medicine researchers at the London School of Economics examined the relationship between volunteering and measures of happiness in a large group of American adults, they found that the more often people volunteered, the happier they were. Compared with people who never volunteered, the odds of being "very happy" rose 7 percent among those who volunteer monthly, and 12 percent for people who volunteer every two to four weeks. Among weekly volunteers, 16 percent felt very happy — a hike in happiness comparable to having an income of $75,000–$100,000 versus $20,000 say the researchers.[26]

Remember that social trait of Lucky people? One of the best ways to make new friends and strengthen existing relationships is to commit to a shared activity. Volunteering is a great way to meet a variety of people, especially if you are new to an area. Volunteering builds connections and is a wonderful way to meet like-minded people, gain a sense of belonging, and build life-long friendships. It strengthens your ties to the community and broadens your support network, exposing you to folk with common interests, neighborhood resources, and fun and fulfilling activities. Linking people to each other, to organizations, and to information is critical to improving our quality of life.

"While some people are naturally outgoing, others are shy and have a hard time meeting new people. Volunteering gives you the opportunity to practice and develop your social skills since you are meeting regularly with a group of people with common interests. Once you have momentum, it's easier to branch out to make more friends and contacts." [27]

Often boards and committees are made up of the wealthy and successful. An excellent path to possible future employment or business is to develop a relationship with the board members.

Do you like to give away things? Give away your aches and pains! One excellent benefit of volunteering is that people who volunteer tend to experience fewer aches and pains. Engaging in acts of kindness produces endorphins, the brain's natural painkiller. Volunteering protects overall health twice as much as aspirin protects against heart disease. How about these lucky seniors? People 55 plus who volunteer in two or more organizations have a forty-four percent lower likelihood of dying early.[28] That is a stronger effect than exercising four times per week. How lucky is that! Especially if you hate to exercise. Now you can just volunteer for two or more organizations.

George Kaiser, one of the richest people in the world and one of the top fifty American philanthropists has been quoted as saying that his good fortune was due to dumb luck, not superior moral character. This advantage is the reason for his charitable commitment.

BE A CAT

Take a cat nap! Oh yes, you read that correctly. We nappers are now pumping our fists in victory. I have always been a napper. It wasn't a want. It wasn't a desire. It was a need. I would return home from work, (barely able to keep my eyes open), hit the couch, nap for ten or fifteen glorious minutes and pop up refreshed. Serendipitously, I was even napping correctly.

Pay attention, all you nap haters. I was amazed to learn there are such people. Who doesn't like a delicious nap? People who are doing it wrong, that's who. The no-no nap-naysayers are getting two things wrong. They are napping for too long a time, and they are "caffinating" wrong.

Nap studies-yes, they are a thing and wouldn't you like to be a participant-have shown that naps of 10-20 minutes are best.[29] These quick naps produce the most benefits in terms of reduced sleepiness and improved cognition. Naps of thirty minutes or longer are likely to be accompanied by what is termed 'sleep inertia' which is the period of cold water splashing, face slapping, caffeine guzzling that follows a 'too long' nap. Sleep inertia is the confused feeling, the grogginess and disorientation one may experience after a long nap.

Next, have a nappucino. Could this study get any better! It may seem counterintuitive, but caffeine takes about twenty minutes to kick in; therefore, drinking a cup of coffee or tea before a nap ensures that your jolt of java will begin to do its thing just as you are waking up.

Find your 'nappy' happy place. For the perfect nap, research suggests lying down in a quiet, dark place and using a sleep mask and earplugs, if necessary. For me, a couch nap takes it, hands down.

But why should we nap at all? Are you working the old 9 to 5? Then you are probably familiar with the mid-afternoon slump-the point when you crash. The sugar rush and high-octane coffee are no longer powering that early morning, 'I'm going to get so much done today!'

Many of the high-tech companies are now recognizing employees' health and as a consequence, the importance of sleep, as one of the best predictors of a company's health. Google, one of these companies, has many times been named the best company to work for.

Google's Vice-President of Real Estate and Workplace Service, David Radcliffe, says, "No workplace is complete without a nap pod. We found that the five-minute to fifteen-minute power nap works on Sunday before you watch the football game, so why not here at work?" [30]

Naps can restore alertness, enhance performance, and reduce mistakes and accidents. A study at NASA on sleepy military pilots and astronauts found that a forty-minute nap improved performance by 34 percent and alertness by 100 percent.[31]

Naps can increase alertness in the period directly following the nap and may extend sharpness a few more hours later in the day.

In his book '***When: The Scientific Secrets of Perfect Timing***', Daniel H. Pink[32] refers to a University of California-Berkeley Study in which nappers easily outperformed non-nappers in retaining information. The study showed an afternoon nap expands the brain's capacity to learn. I knew I loved napping-er 'learning.'

Daniel H. Pink references other studies that show that napping:

- » Leads to benefits in terms of mood, alertness, and cognitive performance.
- » Is beneficial to performance on tasks that include addition, logical reasoning and reaction time.
- » Increases 'flow'-a source of engagement and creativity.
- » Strengthens our immune system and reduces blood pressure.

» Boosts short-term memory as well as associative memory, which is the type of memory that allows us to match a face to a name.

» Nappers are twice as likely to solve a complex problem than those who hadn't napped.

Nappers, could we get any luckier! Not only can we now justify napping, we can also increase our work performance. We will be more alert, react more quickly, solve complex problems, and be less stressed while doing it. Plus, won't our clients be impressed when we remember their names. I'm off to have a nap.

> Always Nap When You Can.
> It is Cheap Medicine
>
> **LORD BYRON**

LUCKY LEARNING

- Lucky people model successful people.
- The early bird wins- Waking up early has numerous benefits.
- Watch your waistline.
- Vigorous exercise slows aging.
- Weight training and resistance training have significant benefits.
- Take advantage of the many benefits of meditation, which can be a keystone habit.
- The super successful read non-fiction every day.
- Reading books can increase your lifespan and improve your cognitive abilities.
- Wealthy people are more likely to read than those with lower incomes.
- Engage in new, stimulating activities.
- Make your bed. Making your bed is a keystone habit that instills a sense of pride.
- Pay yourself first. Save by not spending. Look for small ways to save money.
- Take note. Those who are millionaires are 289 percent more likely to maintain a calendar and a to-do-list than those who are less affluent.

- Pay attention to serendipitous moments to take advantage of the opportunities they provide. We may then interpret these events as lucky. Create a coincidence journal.

- Recording feelings of gratitude can reduce aches and pains, improve sleep quality, increase happiness, and reduce loneliness.

- Volunteer. Many super successful people volunteer as least five hours a month.

- Volunteering increases happiness, builds connections and life-long friendships.

- Take a cat nap of 10-20 minutes. Naps can restore alertness, enhance performance and help us retain information.

MY LUCKY HABIT ACTION PLAN

1.

2.

3.

4.

5.

6.

CHAPTER 7

HEALTHY BODY, HEALTHY MIND, HEALTHY BANK ACCOUNT

I Get Enough Exercise Just by Pushing My Luck!

Lucky for Us! Exercising is the Wise Thing to Do.

Exercise won't make you superhuman, but it can make you smarter. Data from research found a convincing link between cardiovascular health and performance on IQ tests. Researchers observed that young adults between the ages of 15 to 18 who improved their cardiovascular health also saw an increase in their IQ.[1]

Executive functions are your higher-level thinking skills. These include attention, goal management, inhibition control and task switching. Such skills are essential for problem-solving, planning, and organizing. Researchers analyzing multiple studies found that exercise is a favorable way for healthy people to optimize their higher order brain functions.[2]

A study conducted at the University of British Columbia found that aerobic exercise boosts the size of the hippocampus, the brain area involved in verbal memory and learning. Studies show that the parts of the brain which control thinking and memory (the prefrontal cortex and medial temporal cortex) have greater volume in people who exercise versus people who don't.[3]

In a Ted Talk[4] on the brain-changing benefits of exercise Wendy Suzuki asserts, "Exercise is the most transformative thing you can do for your brain today." Ms. Suzuki also states that exercise produces new brain cells in the hippocampus, increasing its volume.

LUCKY WORKOUTS FOR WORK

Want to increase your pay, hold a college degree or be creative? Don't just get lucky, get fit. Many studies show a link between fitness and income. One study shows that heading to the gym at least three times per week has been linked to higher pay. The increase was 12 percent higher for women and 7 percent higher for men.[5]

Exercise can have other beneficial effects on your professional life. A study of 200 white-collar workers from three organizations reported several positive effects from working out before work or during their breaks. The results included better mood, better time management, and increased employee tolerance.[6]

If you are looking for an edge at work or an extra boost to impress the boss, exercise in the morning before going to work. Morning workouts spike brain activity, prepare you for the mental stresses of the day, increase retention of new information, and provide better reaction to complex situations.

Perhaps those who do work out feel more inspired. Research shows that "those who exercise on a regular basis are more productive and have more energy than their sedentary peers." This same study shows that a cardio session can boost creativity for up to two hours afterwards. Exercise outdoors and boost your self-esteem at the same time.[7]

Exercise might even make you age more slowly. Plus, aerobic exercise helps improve the look of your skin. Your fat cells will shrink. Aren't we lucky! All we have to do is dance, or go for a hike or swim and we get happier, smarter and younger looking!

> Luck is the Dividend of Sweat.
> The More You Sweat the Luckier You Get.
> RAY KROC

As luck will have it, while you are getting younger, smarter and better looking, you are also putting in the 10,000 hours it takes to achieve mastery in a field. In his 2008 book "*Outliers*" Malcolm Gladwell[8] wrote that "Ten thousand hours is the magic number of greatness." This quote has been the basis for a great extent of discussion, including that of popular music lyrics. Macklemore and Ryan Lewis wrote a song about it, *Ten Thousand Hours*.

Whether you want to be a champion in sports or a famous artist, don't just push your luck, create it. Good things often don't happen by chance-the best things happen to the people who put in the time and effort. It takes years of practice to become an overnight sensation. Success takes effort. From the ages of seven and eight years old Venus and Serena Williams, professional American tennis players and multi Grand Slam title winners, woke up at 6 a.m. to hit the courts to practice. Success also takes determination. Michael Jordan was cut from his high school basketball team. As we know, he didn't give up.

One thing these champions and others have in common is willpower. Willpower is another skill closely related to executive function. We use willpower to help us stay on track with our goals and stick to our habits. Remember Chapter 5 and how we develop our habits? A study in the British Journal of Sports Medicine looked at several groups of people. The study found "that short bouts of exercise had a significant affect across *all* age groups in areas of executive function, along with inhibition and interference control – which is better known as willpower."[9] Exercise helps increase your willpower. Now you just need the willpower to exercise!

A study published in the New England Journal of Medicine reported on the effects of recreational activities on mental acuity in aging. The objective of the study was to see if any physical or cognitive recreational activities influenced mental acuteness. Some of the cognitive exercises had a beneficial effect on mental acuity: reading reduces risk of dementia by 35 percent and doing crossword puzzles at least four days a week offers protection against dementia by 47 percent.[10] If you like to dance, you have just hit the luck and exercise jackpot. Sorry, golfers. You are out of luck. As are bicyclers and swimmers. When it comes to aging, you need to be less like Tiger and Michael and more like Bruno Mars. The winner of the physical activity jackpot was frequent dancing; which reduces the risk of dementia by 76 percent.[11] Dancing integrates several brain functions at once, increasing your connectivity. Dancing simultaneously involves kinesthetic, rational, musical and emotional processes. Ballroom dancing is a fun workout activity with both physical and mental demands that have a higher impact on cognitive functioning than just exercise or mental tasks alone. Ballroom dancing requires that we integrate different parts of the brain such as strategy, coordination and rhythm.

LUCKY CENTENARIANS

People who live a very long life got lucky in the gene pool. Or did they? It turns out they may have had a little help. Evidence keeps mounting that exercise is a lucky boon for the brain. It can lower a person's risk for Alzheimer's disease and may slow brain aging by about ten years.[12]

Recent technology has given scientists the tools to study the mechanisms involved in the cognitive declines that often come with age. "Aerobic exercise appears to lead to changes in both the structure of the brain and the way it operates, which together bolster learning in kids, give adults an edge on cognitive tasks and protect against the cognitive declines that often come with age."[13]

> "Your body achieves only what
> your mind believes!"
>
> **UNKNOWN**

Here are some ways that exercise helps you get lucky and fit for a ripe old age:[14]

- » Lowers your chances of heart disease.
- » Reduces your odds of having diabetes, colon cancer, and osteoporosis.
- » Keeps your bones, muscles, and joints healthy.
- » Lowers your blood pressure.
- » Helps manage stress and improve your mood.
- » Eases symptoms of anxiety and depression.
- » Helps manage chronic conditions like arthritis or diabetes by helping with things like stamina, joint swelling, pain, and muscle strength.
- » Helps with your balance, so you're less likely to fall and break bones.

> You can't help getting older,
> but you don't have to get old.
>
> **GEORGE BURNS**

LUCKY LEARNING

- » Optimize your higher order brain functions through exercise.

- » You might increase your IQ through exercise as the prefrontal cortex and medial temporal cortex have greater volume in people who exercise versus people who don't.

- » Heading to the gym has been linked to higher pay.

- » Exercising before work has positive effects such as better mood, better time management, and increased employee tolerance.

- » Exercise increases retention of information, spikes brain activity, provides exercisers with more energy than sedentary peers and boosts creativity.

- » Exercise has a significant effect on executive function, along with inhibition and willpower.

- » Dance, dance, dance. Dancing is likely the best workout activity with both physical and mental benefits.

- » Reduce your risk of Alzheimer's disease through exercise.

MY LUCKY HABITS

1.

2.

3.

4.

5.

6.

CHAPTER 8

OLD HABITS DO DIE HARD

Those who keep old habits die hard and young!

Is it one in the morning and you are eating that "last" chocolate chip cookie one "last" time? Are you late (once again) because you hit that snooze button too many times (once again)? Are you standing in front of the fridge door at one in the morning? You are not alone. According to research reported in the Journal of Clinical Psychology[1], 54 percent of people who determine to change a habit fail to make the resolution last beyond six months. Even more shocking, the average person makes the same resolution ten times without success.

Psychologists believe we need to work with our brain rather than fight against it. Remember how we needed a reward to establish our good habits? Bad habits also generally reward you with something - an urge is satisfied: eating a cookie tastes delicious and gives you a sugar rush, smoking gives you stress release, and wasting time on the internet diverts your attention, as well as making you feel connected. Biting your nails releases stress, as do many other bad habits. The next time you try to turn an unfortunate habit into a lucky trait, try these psychology-based approaches.[2]

1. **Identify your bad habits.** Pinpointing our bad habits is a first step toward eliminating those vices. Keeping a journal is one of the practices of lucky people. Journaling helps you build better habits as it forces you to be aware of your actions and behaviors. Increase Awareness - Put It in Writing. Keep track of what you were doing before and after the undesired behavior, what time of day the action occurred or occurs, where the behavior transpired and identify who you were with.

2. **Pinpoint how bad habits reward you.** Does the habit release stress? Make you feel happy? Often habits release a chemical called dopamine, which creates the craving to do it again. While identifying undesired actions and journaling about them, determine how they make you feel, as well.

3. **Identify triggers.** Do you drink more alcohol when you are around specific people? Do you overeat when you watch T.V. at night? Do you smoke as soon as you get in your car or right after a meal? Knowing what triggers and rewards the unwanted behaviors can help identify strategies for changing these unhealthy patterns.

4. **Find a replacement habit.** Bad habits provide benefits and fulfill particular needs in your life. It is far more effective

to replace a bad habit with a new practice or routine than to try to stop performing the old habit. If you attempt to cut out the undesired behavior without replacing it, you'll have unmet needs. Plan your substitute habit. Strategize ahead of time how you will respond to the urge to smoke, bite your nails, check your email, watch mindless T.V., or hit the snooze button.

5. Depending on the habit you are trying to remove, here are a few suggestions:

   » Prepare fruit or vegetables ahead of time so that they are handy and easy to reach for instead of junk food. Freeze bite-sized chunks of fruit to munch on instead of candy. Frozen grapes are delicious.

   » Go for a walk. Doing so prevents overeating, drinking, binge-watching T.V. and many other undesired indulgences.

   » Get a dog. The dog will get you up early to prevent you from hitting the snooze button, and your pet will need walking, causing you to exercise more.

   » Join a group of friends who don't smoke or binge out on junk food (or whatever habit you are trying to break) and who like to do another activity which you enjoy.

   » If you are trying to become an early-riser, a Lucky Trait, join a group of friends (or just one friend) who are morning larks and like to do an activity you savor.

6. **Eliminate your triggers.** When trying to quit smoking, drinking or eating junk food, you should remove the

temptations from the house. If binge-watching is your vice, put the remote in a closet in another room. You will need to think about going to get the remote which gives you a chance to replace the behavior.

7. **Change your environment or routine.** New routines or situations make you more conscious of your habits and behavior choices. The change in pattern does not have to be directly related to the habit you are trying to break. Ending relationships or moving are often accompanied by small changes such as more frequent exercise or a new diet. Place your alarm clock (or phone) on the other side of the room, away from your bed. You will need to get out of bed to turn off the alarm. If you overeat while watching T.V., sit at a table and turn off the T.V. while eating. Keep your cigarettes outside so that you need to go out to smoke, causing you to think about the behavior.

8. **Visualize yourself succeeding.** Picture yourself doing an alternative activity. Envision yourself breaking the bad habit by removing the triggers. Imagine yourself successful, achieving your goal. For example, see yourself waking up early, stretching your arms over your head, getting out of bed, immediately donning some work-out clothes and going for a walk or run. Research shows that the neural synapses that fire when we perform an activity, are the same as those that fire when we envision performing that identical behavior.[2] By conceptualizing your ideal circumstance, you'll help yourself achieve it.

LUCKY LEARNING

- » Increase awareness of bad habits by putting them in writing.
- » Pinpoint how bad habits reward you.
- » Identify triggers.
- » Find replacement behaviors.
- » Avoid/remove triggers.
- » Change your environment or routine.
- » Visualize success.

VISUALIZATION

Go to your favorite spot. Perhaps the one you use for meditation. The spot with no noise, no interruptions. See yourself learning the steps of your new lucky habit. Mentally practice the good behavior over the bad. Visualize yourself succeeding in your fresh endeavor.

UNLUCKY OLD HABITS

UNLUCKY OLD HABITS I WANT TO BREAK:

1.
   - » The Habit: _____
   - » The Reward: _____
   - » The Trigger: _____
   - » The Lucky Habit Replacement: _____
   _____

2.
   - » The Habit: _____
   - » The Reward: _____
   - » The Trigger: _____
   - » The Lucky Habit Replacement: _____
   _____

CHAPTER 9

TEAM LUCK-GOAL SETTING

We have all heard the expression we are what we eat. By now you may have realized we are also what we repeatedly do. Now that we know what to do to kick our bad habits and to set some good practices, we are going to ensure even more luck by focusing on our life's goals. Goal setting is crucial to success. The rich and famous set goals. The innovators set goals. The lucky ones set goals.

Tony Robbins says that the root of success is having goals. Goals are fundamental to success.[1] Likely you have set goals in the past. We have all set goals.

But what is goal setting? Goal setting is everywhere. The self-help gurus talk about goal setting. Bookstores have whole sections on goal setting. A Google search reveals hundreds of hits. Everywhere we look, wherever we go, we are encouraged to set goals. But what is goal setting and why should we set goals?

Seth Godin, bestselling writer and blogger, says that people who lead and make an impact have goals. People who have goals are the people who get things done.[2]

Brian Tracy is recognized as a top authority in sales training and personal success and is the author of the bestseller *The Psychology of Achievement*. In his blog post, Positive Affirmations and Long-Term Goals Change Your Luck[3], Mr. Tracy writes that the key to having more luck is to engage in additional actions that result in your desired consequences. You can bring about the chosen results through your long-term goals. Success is largely under your control through goal-setting and self-improvement. To rephrase Sir Isaac Newton's Law of Action and Reaction-for every action there is an equal and opposite reaction-actions have consequences. Mr. Tracy propounds success is not a matter of luck at all; rather, success is the effect of one's goals and actions.

> By having long-term goals you will create your own luck through positive affirmations, goal setting, and self-improvement.

Your goal is the result you want. Goal setting is the system you will use to set the direction to achieve the goal. Perhaps you want to run a marathon, write a book, or travel to twenty-five countries. If you're going to run a marathon, your goal setting or system is the training schedule you set. Writing a book? Your goal setting is your daily writing schedule. Traveling to twenty-five countries? Your goal-setting becomes more complicated. You may first need to set goals for raising funds. Next, you may want to set goals for quitting your job or obtaining employment in some or all of the countries you are visiting. Maybe you will set goals for establishing an on-line business you can do anywhere. Your goal tells you what type of system or systems you need to put in place. Pretend you are a pelican. Your goal is that delicious, salty grouper you see swimming around in the ocean below. With your super keen eyesight you zero in, set your goal systems (targeting, wing-flapping, diving) and success- a tasty lunch! I am writing this on my balcony overlooking the ocean in Florida. Spending the winters in Florida was a previous goal of mine.

Know the benchmark of success. Whatever your goal is, you will be more effective in achieving it if your goal meets precise criteria:

- » **Specific**- Instead of saying, "I want to increase my daily walking," rephrase it to say, "I want to increase my daily walking to 10,000 steps by May 1." Or instead of "increased sales" make it "a twenty-five percent increase in sales over last year."

- » **Measurable**- Smart goals are measurable-steps, sales, weight loss, countries visited, number of reps, fewer cigarettes smoked, etc.

- » **Attainable**- Your goal must be realistic. Set goals in small steps or chunks to make them more achievable and more successful. Do not set yourself up for failure. For example, instead of just wanting to lose fifty pounds, set a goal of losing five pounds in one month. Eat vegetarian every

Tuesday. Save five percent of your salary for six months and then increase it to ten percent.

- » **Timely**- Set a time to achieve the goal. One month, six months, a year.

BE THE TORTOISE, NOT THE HARE

Remember to keep your goals optimistic, but realistic. Successful people have a long-term mindset. They think big but chunk it small. Focus on the small steps. Mini-increments make the largest gains in the long term. Conjure up your grit. No, I don't mean grit your teeth, although you may have to do that, too. Google defines "grit" as courage, resolve, pluck, mettle, and backbone. Hang in there and keep moving forward.

RECORDING YOUR GOALS

Is there a perfect way, a successful way to record your goals? Educators are taught that we all learn differently, that we have various modalities for learning, some stronger than others. One person's preferred way of learning might be visual while another person's style of learning might be kinesthetic. Your personal rituals strengthen your beliefs. Just as everyone learns differently, there isn't one perfect goal-setting system. Here are some ideas for recording your goal-setting.

VISUAL WAYS TO DO GOAL SETTING

- » Stick photos of your goal everywhere. Remember my weight loss and work out photos on my fridge?
- » Scroll your goal across your computer screen saver.

- » Write your goal on a Post-it note and stick it on your bathroom mirror to ensure you see it first thing in the morning.

- » Create Pinterest Boards related to your goals and check them daily.

- » Create a vision board.

- » Share your goal with the world-or at least with your online friends. On New Year's Day, your birthday, or some other significant date, post your goal on your Facebook page or your Instagram page.

WRITE YOUR GOALS

People who write their goals *accomplish significantly more* than those who do not write their goals.

A study by the Dominican University of California[4] found those who wrote down their goals, committed to action and regularly sent updates to a peer, were the most successful in attaining their goals. Dr. Gail Matthews, a psychology professor at the Dominican University of California, discovered those who write down their goals on a regular basis are 42 percent more likely to achieve their goals.

> Goals are like magnets. They attract the things that make them come true.
>
> **TONY ROBBINS**

PHYSICAL WAYS TO DO GOAL SETTING

» Write a daily journal entry about your goal. Research shows that the brain is the most creative and active following sleep. Use this burst of creative energy to record and review your goals.

» Include statements about why you want to meet that goal, what its benefits are, what steps you will take, how you will measure the goal, and how success will look.

» Tweet your goal-The physical act of succinctly stating your goal in 280 characters or fewer will help you refine your goal.

» Create a daily gratitude dairy or log, thanking God, the universe, Buddha or your supreme being for your increased luck, new found wealth, weight loss, better health, travels, etc. Robert Emmons[5], a University of California professor, conducted research in which he found that participants who kept gratitude lists were more likely to have made progress toward important personal goals (academic, interpersonal and health-based) over a two-month period compared to subjects in the other experimental conditions.

» If your goal is a new house, and you have one in mind, drive by it every day.

» If you are trying to walk or run a certain daily distance, add a marker that indicates that specific, targeted distance. For example, tie a tiny ribbon on a tree branch on the one-mile or one K mark. Do this for every mile or kilometer.

AUDIO WAYS TO DO GOAL SETTING

» Record your goal onto your smartphone. You can replay the recording for goal reminders and motivation.

» Become the drama queen or king you always wanted to be. Write a mini-play about achieving your goal(s). Act it out for your friends and family.

VISUALIZATION

We have all heard the adage 'seeing is believing.' Perhaps the **Lucky Ones** see better than others. Luck is something you create and attract. Individuals who have the luck of the Irish visualize what they want and then venture forth and achieve just that in the real world. The super successful understand that what they can envision in their minds, they can achieve in the physical world.

Visualization is a technique in which you picture yourself accomplishing something you want. When thinking about visualization, conjure up a picture of Clydesdale draught horses. See them harnessed to the power of your subconscious mind.

Visualization is a concept that has been used by athletes for many years. It is an integral part of sports psychology which helps athletes and others improve their performance and actualize their goals. According to an article in the Huffington Post[6], visualization works because neurons in our brains decode imagery as analogous to the main event. Due to recently developed brain imagery we can see how visualization works. The brain generates an impulse that commands our neurons to "perform" the movement. Our brain has now created a new neural pathway-a cluster of cells in our brain that network to create learned behaviors or memories. Psychologists have discovered that visualizing the activity has almost the same effect as performing the action.

In the Introduction we read about Jim Carrey living in a van and dropping out of school to make ends meet. But did you know that in 1985, that same young, impoverished Jim Carrey famously wrote himself a check for $10 million for "acting services rendered," dated it for 1994, and carried it in his wallet for daily inspiration? In 1994, Carrey made precisely $10 million for his starring role in Dumb and Dumber, and tens of millions more thereafter.

Sara Blakely, the self-made billionaire, once had a small, disruptive idea to cut off the feet of her control-top pantyhose, which led her to patent her own footless, body shaping pantyhose and ultimately led to her billion-dollar business, Spanx. Blakely once envisioned herself on Oprah's couch even though she was unsure of the reason why and years later, Oprah named Spanx one of her favorite things of 2000. In an interview on money.cnn.com, Blakely said she had been manifesting and visualizing a different life for herself. Ms. Blakely stated she specifically wrote down in her journal that she wanted to invent something she could sell to millions of people and she wanted the product to make people feel good.[7]

Sara's story is also one of determination and preparation. She was determined to succeed and prepared to do the work it took to make that success happen. In the same interview with CNN, Sara stated that finding a manufacturer was difficult. She was turned down by mill after mill. Sara expressed that every time she heard a *no*, she just kept going.

Motivational speaker, author, and performance coach, Tony Robbins, has a ten-minute morning routine that he calls priming. Priming includes breathing exercises, meditation, expressing gratitude and visualization. The last three minutes of Robbins' morning routine are spent visualizing what it is like to achieve a goal. Robbins suggests to not think about making it happen but to see your goal as completed. To achieve success in both finance and life, envisioning goals is crucial. Tony Robbins runs and repeats incantations to himself to stay focused on his goals.[8]

> Always discover your vision
> and the rest will follow.
> ARNOLD SCHWARZENEGGER

It is time to don your Super Luck Hero costume from Chapter 3. Now we're at the juncture where it's time to visualize and design your lucky life. To what do you aspire? What do you hunger for? What is your coveted goal? You must be definitive about what you desire. The critical luck factor here is clarity. You must be absolutely clear about what you want. Engage in an elevated level of action to achieve your goal. How does one accomplish this? Luckily, the internet and bookstores are replete with instructions and how-to manuals that can provide in-depth training and tutelage for those who wish to dive deep into the luck well and find the pot of gold at the bottom. If you are wearing your Lucky Luck costume, if your Clydesdale is hitched and eager to trot, here are a few suggestions to get started.

ESTABLISH YOUR GOAL OR DESIRE

Start small. Lose one belt size. Get one free-lance job. Sell one photograph. What? Whoa! Hold that Clydesdale. Jim Carrey didn't start small. Sarah Blakely didn't start small. You won't for long, either. The idea is to create a few victories to feel the power of the win. Rehearsing success will help you feel more motivated to go for the big one.

Be 'Senseational.' Create a vision using all your senses. If your goal is something you want to do better, create a mental movie of yourself being more skillful at doing that thing. Use as much detail as you can imagine. How do you look? What are you wearing? What is the expression on your face? Where are you? What is the environment like? What does it smell like? Look like? Sound like? Use all your senses to imagine yourself achieving your ultimate success. This technique is also suitable for creating visions for travel. Create a mental movie of yourself in the country, city, town, lake, resort, etc. that you want to visit. Imagine yourself swimming, boating, skiing, eating, touring, sightseeing or volunteering there. Envision your dream activity and place.

Say Cheese. If your goal is an object, create a photograph or picture of yourself with your goal as if it is already achieved. If you have a dream house in mind, take a selfie in front of that house. Is there a specific new car you want? Go down to the dealership. Sit behind the wheel and have a friend take a picture of you. Want to go to Paris? Print a photo of the Eiffel Tower and paste a photograph of yourself in front of it-or photo-shop yourself into the picture.

Ask for what you want. Both through manifestation and in reality. Make requests. What is the worst that can happen? Maybe the people in your life don't know that is your desire.

LUCKY LEARNING

- » Your goal is the result you want.

- » Goal setting is the system you will use to set the direction to achieve the goal.

- » Know the benchmark of success. Goals should be: **specific, measurable, attainable, timely.**

- » Think big but chunk small.

- » Record your goals.

- » Visualize your goals-start small, be 'senseational,' create a photograph or picture of yourself achieving the goal, ask for what you want.

MY LUCKY GOALS

GOAL 1:

My Goal: _____

Method for Recording My Goal: _____

_____

GOAL 2:

My Goal: _____

Method for Recording My Goal: _____

_____

Section Three

ALL KINDS OF LUCK

ARE WE BORN LUCKY?

GOOD LUCK OR BAD LUCK

TURN BAD LUCK INTO GOOD

A LUCKY BET

CHAPTER 10

ARE WE BORN LUCKY?

May the luck be with you.

Counting your lucky stars? You might have been born in May. Or perhaps June through August. Did you know that some birth dates are luckier bets than others? Richard Wiseman, author of *The Luck Factor*, concluded there is a direct link between the time of year people are born and how lucky they feel. Richard Wiseman and colleagues asked a group of British study participants if they considered themselves lucky. The study also assessed key personality traits. Across genders and ages, spring and summer babies-people born between March and August-feel luckier, on average, than fall and winter babies.[1]

Professor Wiseman suggests environmental factors at the time of birth affect the body's biological system, such as the amount of sunshine and temperature, and that these could affect a person into adulthood.[2] The outcomes may also be due to the way parents and others interact with their babies during summer and winter. Summer babies might be around happier people who are out enjoying the sunlight. Those born in the darker winter months tend to have a gloomier outlook on life. Relatedly, summer babies grow up to be more open-minded and less neurotic than winter tots. May is the luckiest month of all, so if you want a fortunate child, try to get lucky in August.

In a relatively new field, scientists are just beginning to look into birth "seasons" and health. As reported in an article in Business Insider,[3] Columbia University researchers analyzed 175 million patient records. Here is what they found regarding birth month and disease risk. Those born in October and November were most likely to get sick, especially from respiratory diseases. Neurological and reproductive disorders weren't very kind to November babies. Heart-related conditions are higher in those born in March. May and July babies had the lowest risk of illness. As we have been learning, though, we can control our luck, as diet and exercise still play a critical role in our health.

A unique personality type-hyperthymia-is described as being excessively positive with high energy and enthusiasm for life activities. Don't cheer too loudly, but March, April, May babies you score high on the hyperthymia scale. However, there is a downside to your luck. Seemingly contradictory, May babies also score high for clinical depression. November babies, it is your turn to celebrate as those born in November have the lowest rates of depression.

Don't be SAD. It's glad tidings for those born in August as they have the lowest diagnoses of bipolar disorder. Fall babies can also be happy; they enjoy low levels of depression even if they can be a wee bit irritable.

Want your child to be an artist, writer, designer or someone who can save the world? Have a January or February baby. These months correlate with creativity and problem-solving.[4]

There is a captivating story about how Pablo Picasso, the famous Spanish artist, developed the ability to produce remarkable work in just minutes.

As the story goes, Picasso was walking through the market one day when a woman spotted him. She stopped the artist, pulled out a piece of paper and said, "Mr. Picasso, I am a fan of your work. Please, could you do a little drawing for me?"

Picasso smiled and quickly drew a small, but beautiful piece of art on the paper. Then, he handed the paper back to her saying, "That will be one million dollars."

"But Mr. Picasso," the woman said. "It only took you thirty seconds to draw this little masterpiece."

"My good woman," Picasso said, "It took me thirty years to draw that masterpiece in thirty seconds."

Picasso isn't the only brilliant creative who worked for decades to master his craft. His journey is typical of many geniuses. Even people of considerable talent rarely produce incredible work before decades of practice.

> I believe that "luck" is one of the most misunderstood and underappreciated factors in life.
>
> RICHARD BRANSON

Richard Branson tells a story where he was watching the final round of the British Open golf championships on TV. Sir Branson recalls that one of the commentary team exclaimed, "Oh my goodness, what a lucky shot. Another commentator, a retired American Champion snapped back, "Lucky! What do you mean 'lucky'? Do you know how many thousands of hours we all spend practicing shots like that? He was trying to put it in the hole, and he succeeded. Let me tell you; he worked long and hard on getting that lucky!"

Sir Branson says that he, too, has often been accused of being lucky in business, but he states much hard work has played a significant part in any luck that has come his way. Sir Branson admits to being unsure where coincidence stops and good luck begins.

Do you have to have been born a genius to be lucky? Apparently not. In his book, *Outliers*,[5] in the chapter titled 'The Trouble with Geniuses,' Gladwell states that most estimates put the heritability of IQ at roughly 50 percent. Don't despair. Even though you may be the only person who considers yourself a genius, you can still be lucky. Economist James Heckman[6] asked the question, "How much does innate intelligence determine a child's future success?" In other words, how much of the difference between people's incomes can be tied to IQ? Just in case you are wondering why the guy down the street has the big fancy house with the kidney shaped pool and you have the small bungalow with the above ground pool, you can stop panicking. It's not about your IQ. (Well, it might be. Ask your mother or your spouse.) Most people guess the connection is approximately twenty-five percent. But we're in luck. Heckman says the data suggests a much smaller influence: only one or two percent.

In **Chapter 4** I wrote about the traits of successful people. Heckman states that grades and achievement test results are better indicators of adult success than IQ scores. If it is not IQ, does Heckman agree with these traits? He adds non-cognitive skills to the list. These include perseverance and the ability to collaborate. Haven't we seen just these qualities before? Perseverance? Those who succeeded despite hardships and hard-luck stories growing up had to try and try again and not give up. The ability to collaborate? Networking and being social are repeatedly mentioned. Heckman also includes good study habits. We may or may not be born lucky, but recall that many of our habits do come from our parents. Let's not forget, though, that today's titans develop and follow uncannily similar routines on a daily basis. These are habits that the innovators have learned from other successful people and have made it a practice to develop these habits or rituals.

Let's think about athletes for a moment. At first glance, it would seem that some of the top athletes were born incredibly lucky. But perhaps not. An inquiry into Serena Williams' early life reveals that she and her sisters were raised in the economically depressed and often violence-riddled Los Angeles suburb of Compton. Various biographies show Serena on the courts as early as three or four years old, practicing for up to two hours per day. Sound lucky? Brazilians are legends in the soccer world and legend has it that Pele was so impoverished that he first learned the sport by playing soccer with a rolled-up sock stuffed with old rags. Recall what Richard Branson pointed out. A lot of hard work helped create their luck. Just imagine the ten thousand times their feet or hands have touched the ball, their hands have touched the bat or racket, or their body has moved through the water. Through deliberate practice and striving, these athletes lived comedian Steve Martin's motto: *"Become so good they can't ignore you."*

Having said the above, certain athletes may have been born fortuitous. Michael Phelps, lauded by some to perhaps be the greatest athlete of all time, is one. Research reveals several physical attributes that particularly suit Phelps to swimming. He has a long, thin torso which offers low drag. Science says "good" drag comes from thrust force. Thrust force is created by the swimmer's hand moving backward through the water and kicking their feet. Mr. Phelps also has relatively short legs which lower drag and his size 14 feet provide the effect of flippers. Have you ever seen a photo of Michael Phelps' hands and feet?

If only I had known about drag when I was young! I am an excellent swimmer, and I have long, flat feet. Oh, the times I have been teased about my feet. When I snorkel, I sometimes choose not to use flippers. I often joke that I bring my own flippers.

Michael also has an arm span of 6 feet 7 inches (201 cm) – disproportionate to his height of 6 feet 4 inches (193 cm). This means his arms act as propulsive paddles.[7]

Simone Biles is the most decorated American gymnast. Some refer to her as the greatest gymnast ever. Simone has very short arms and legs suitable for tricky rotations. She also has an exceptionally high strength to weight ratio.[8]

Chris Froome, a Tour de France champion, at 6'1 and 147 pounds is super tall and very skinny. He has a very high power to weight ratio. Business Insider says Chris has a very high VO2 max of 88.2, near the peak of what we think is possible for humans, which means he can use oxygen far more efficiently than the average person.[9]

Certainly, there are many more people out there apart from Michael and myself with big feet. Others may have extra-long arms. Some have particularly short arms. Many others are tall and skinny. Do we still consider them lucky? Perhaps we should consider them unlucky? Lazy? Have they been given a unique body type and have not utilized it? Or did fate or other circumstances intervene? Perhaps there wasn't a swimming pool or gymnastics gym within fifty kilometers, or maybe they couldn't afford the admission fee.

As a teenager, Phelps idolized Australian swimmer Ian Thorpe. Just before the 2008 Summer Olympics, Thorpe initially said it would be highly unlikely for Phelps to win eight gold medals. Phelps taped Thorpe's words to his locker during the games as motivation. Michael did win eight gold medals that year. Ultimately, throughout his career, Michael won twenty-three gold medals and twenty-eight overall. Phelps had a rigorous training schedule, not taking a day off in five years.[10]

Although Kenya is a beautiful place, it is not likely that anyone would say most Kenyans are born lucky. Many people who live there are impoverished and work hard. Often it is subsistence living. Few Kenyans receive any sports training, although many young Kenyans do run to school and back. Yet here they are, winning marathon after marathon. Two separate European studies found that in a small region in western Kenya that produces most of the winners, there appeared to be a physical, possibly genetic advantage. Kenyans have less mass for their height, longer legs, shorter torsos, and more slender limbs than many other marathoners.[11] Young Kenyans have incredible VO2 (maximum oxygen uptake) that is likely due to a variety of factors. They live at a high altitude and they run constantly. They train hard. Therefore, we could say that some Kenyans are lucky. They develop amazing lung capacity and they can run like a cheetah.

You might be born with veritable luck. You can't train for your genetics and your physical traits. But you can train. You have to earn your success.

The above sentiment would also hold true for life in general. Do you want to develop your abilities in various areas? Train like an Olympian. Develop these abilities through creative visualization and a committed plan along with a routine and hard work.

Some people may be born with luck or privilege, but it may last only for a period of time. It depends on what they do with the opportunity they are given.

CHAPTER 11

GOOD LUCK OR BAD LUCK

Do you sometimes feel you are a hamster stuck in a cage, running around and around in your hamster wheel doing the same thing over and over again with the same unlucky results? Do you sense you are stuck in an unfortunate luck cycle? Perhaps you believe you are alone with your bad fortune. Do you step into your hamster ball every evening and roll down to the local pub? After all, misery loves company. And such esteemed company it is.

> You Never Know What Worse Luck
> Your Bad Luck Has Saved You From.
> CORMAC MCCARTHY

According to Forbes Magazine[1], Dwayne "The Rock" Johnson, was the highest paid actor in the world in 2016 (and again in 2017.) Yet the above quote could be a perfect mantra for Mr. Johnson. Imagine this. The Rock's original dream was to be a professional football player. Before Johnson had major success as both a wrestler and an actor, his dreams were shattered. In August 2017, Dwayne was in Vancouver, British Columbia, Canada. He spent a moment on Instagram to explain why never making it to the NFL was a good thing. Dwayne describes how at age 22 he arrived in Vancouver to play in his first pro football game in the Canadian Football League. Two days later he was cut. His dreams were shattered, and he was sent home with seven bucks in his pocket. Johnson said that "not playing in the NFL was the best thing that never happened." [2] Not making it as a professional player led Dwayne to become one of the greatest professional wrestlers of all time. His acting career seems to have worked out okay, too.

In another example of bad luck being the springboard for good luck, the knighted British fashion icon, Sir Paul Smith, was given his first bicycle at age eleven and he quit school at age fifteen. Sir Paul had dreams of becoming a pro cyclist until a serious crash ended that dream. He spent three months in the hospital. Upon his release, Paul went to a local pub to meet some friends whom he had met in the hospital. One friend was opening a small boutique to sell the clothes she was designing. Sir Paul organized and managed the shop. These friends introduced him to the world of art and fashion. Life designed his luck from there on, and he now owns three hundred fashion shops worldwide.[3]

In author Gretchen Rubin's podcast, Amy Adams, a five-time Academy Award nominee, conveys her disappointment after being fired from a television drama series. However, Amy was then available for a part in the movie *Junebug*. An academy award nomination was the result. Amy's bad luck was also her good luck.[4]

Many of us are alive today due to the accidental life-saving discovery of penicillin. Alexander Fleming's discovery of penicillin in 1928 occurred while he was investigating staphylococcus, a common type of bacteria. While Fleming was away on a two-week vacation, a petri dish containing a staphylococcus culture was left on a lab bench and never placed in the incubator as intended. Somehow, a *Penicillium* mold spore accidentally floated into the medium either through the window or up the stairwell from the lab below. The temperature conditions permitted both the bacteria and the mold spores to grow; had the incubator been used, only the bacteria could have grown. Fleming later made a key observation; an inhibition or prevention of bacterial growth in areas affected by 'mold juice'.[5]

In the Middle of Every Difficulty Lies Opportunity.
ALBERT EINSTEIN

Here is a sweet, good luck tale. Saccharin, the first commercially available artificial sweetener, was discovered by accident. In 1878, Russian chemist Constantin Fahlberg was working in a small lab at the John Hopkins University, experimenting with coal tar derivatives and other projects. One night after leaving the lab, Mr. Fahlberg sat down to dinner after forgetting to wash his hands. Fahlberg noticed that the roll he was eating was extraordinarily sweet tasting. He realized that the sweetness was coming from a residue on his hands. Fahlberg rushed back to the lab and licked various lab instruments to determine the source, eventually discovering a beaker that had boiled over and contained the ingredients. Fahlberg wasn't lucky with the coal tar derivatives that night, but he soon patented the sweet ingredients as saccharin.[6]

While I was writing this book, the 2018 Winter Olympics were taking place. As happens during Olympics, there were many tales of endurance, triumph and broken dreams. For one Canadian figure skater, the 2018 Olympics were the culmination of her aspirations.

In the moments after her bronze medal-winning skate, Kaetlyn Osmond thought of the gruesome broken leg that almost drove her out of the sport, and she was so thankful that it happened.

Osmond said she nearly called it quits and hung up her skates. Ms. Osmond indicated that she felt she would not have been able to perform the way she did without that injury. The injury caused her to regroup and become an almost new person. Kaetlyn divulged that she had to mature and refocus on how to stay strong.[7]

There is a well-known story of a farmer who used an old horse to till his fields. One day the horse escaped into the nearby hills. When the farmer's neighbors sympathized with him over his bad luck the farmer replied, "Bad luck? Good luck? Who knows?"

A while later, the old horse returned with a herd of horses from the hills. This time the neighbors congratulated the farmer on his good luck. Once again, the farmer's reply was, "Bad luck? Good luck? Who knows?"

A while later, while attempting to tame one of the wild horses, the farmer's son fell off the horse and broke his leg. The neighbors thought this was terrible luck. The farmer's reaction: "Bad luck? Good luck? Who knows?"

Weeks later, the army marched into the village and conscripted every able-bodied young man in the village. The farmer's son, with his broken leg, was not recruited. With patience, calm, and acceptance, bad luck continually became good luck.

TURN BAD LUCK INTO GOOD

All of Us Have Bad Luck
ROBERT COLLIER

Robert Collier, a self-help guru who was one of the sources for the famous motivational book, *The Secret*, is often quoted as saying that we all have good and bad luck. We need to persist through the bad luck so that we are there when the good luck comes. We need to be ready to receive it.

Did you know that Warren Buffet was rejected by Harvard Business School? In HBO's '**Becoming Warren Buffet**,' the investor said his first thought was, "What do I tell my dad?" But, he says, "It turned out to be the best thing that ever happened to me." The Harvard rejection led Mr. Buffet to eventually apply to Columbia Business School. Later that summer while flipping through a catalogue for Columbia, Buffett recognized the name of Professor Benjamin Graham, the father of value investing. He had just read Graham's book, *The Intelligent Investor*. Buffet later said that finding that book was one of the luckiest moments of his life. There is an important point to note here. Remember in the habits section above it was noted that successful people mentored and were mentored? Buffet speaks of Benjamin Graham as an incredible teacher who shaped his professional life.

Buffet applied to Columbia and was admitted. The now renowned investor credits Graham with teaching him the two rules of investing that Buffet has lived by throughout his outstanding career. The two rules? Rule number one: Never lose money. Rule number two: Never forget rule number one.[8]

Sara Blakely, the billionaire founder of Spanx, failed the LSAT exam.[9] This meant she could not become a lawyer like her father. Sara next tried out to be Goofy at Disney World, but she was too short! Had Sara been successful at becoming a lawyer, or Goofy, millions of women around the world would be out of shape.

Adam Sicinski of *"How to Attract Good Luck to Achieve Your Goals"* [10] wrote that many people see what seems to be **bad luck** as nothing more than an event inconsequential to their long-term success and happiness. Those who believe in the luck factor set themselves free from misfortune by viewing it in a positive, yet realistic light. Sicinski suggests that individuals blessed with good luck view bad luck as a chance to grow.

As an educator, I see lessons everywhere. When analyzing poor luck, take time to identify the lesson. Ask yourself, "Is there an important message inherent in this?" "What can I learn from this? Is there an adjustment I can make to the plan? A tweak?" You can change your life by changing your thinking.

WHEN THERE'S A WILL, THERE'S A WAY

Do you know a favored someone who is very determined? One lucky charm seems to be that of willpower. The people with the determination to persist in the face of adversity seem to be among the blessed. No matter what challenges they have to push through, their determination to move forward provides them with a vast array of fortitude and luck. We harness our willpower when we resist short-term gratification in exchange for a long-term goal. An article in designluck.com[11] suggests that scientists' new theory of willpower shows willpower as non-limited instead of unlimited. We should view willpower as self-renewing and not limited by the constraints in our head. Research is showing that our day-to-day mindset plays a larger role towards our success than ever assumed.

When life shovels dirt on you-step up. Perhaps you've heard the tale of the donkey and the well. If not, it goes like this.

One day a farmer's donkey fell down a well. The donkey brayed and cried for hours and hours as the farmer tried to figure out what to do. Finally, the farmer came to the decision that the donkey was old and that the well needed to be covered up anyway; it just wasn't worth it to save the donkey. (Who is the real ass here?)

The farmer invited his neighbors to help him. They began to shovel dirt into the well. When the donkey realized what was happening, it brayed and cried horribly. Then after a while, it quieted down. Had it given in to its bad luck?

The farmers and neighbors shoveled some more. After a while, the farmer was astonished by what he saw. As each shovel load of dirt hit his back, the donkey would shake it off and take a step up. Soon everyone was amazed to see the donkey step over the edge of the well and happily trot off.

Moral: Each of our troubles is a stepping stone to higher success. We can get out of the deepest well by never giving up. Shake off bad luck and take a step up.

> The only good luck many great men ever had was being born with the ability and determination to overcome bad luck.
> CHANNING POLLOCK

Lucky people handle adversity differently than unlucky people. When they hit a stumbling block, they're more likely to transform it into a positive event-to reframe their experience. Lucky people do not dwell on their ill fortune; they take productive, encouraging steps to avert more bad luck.

You can't always control what happens to you, but you can control how you react to an event. Boost your success by finding the value in bad luck. Look for the silver lining. If something goes awry, might it be a blessing in disguise? Is it the universe's way of trying to send you in another direction? Playback the situation in your mind. Evaluate your actions and make improvements where needed. Don't wallow in self-pity. Don't dwell on the adverse events. Cultivate a belief that things will get better.

Get busy turning your bad luck into good fortune. See bad luck as a temporary condition. Even if you have had a run of bad luck, you can turn things around. First of all, take a break. Go on a mini-vacation, spend time with friends, see a movie or get some exercise. Perhaps take a step back to put things into perspective.

Develop a problem-solving mindset. Be proactive. Take action to turn your luck around. Increase your sense of personal control.

Create a plan. Brainstorm for all possible options. Be open to every idea. Prioritize ideas. Be sure to take action. A plan without action is just that, a plan.

> Action is the foundational key to all success.
> PABLO PICASSO

Stay flexible and make adjustments as necessary. Could this be a springboard to a newly discovered opportunity?

> A man often meets his destiny
> on the road he took to avoid it.
> JEAN DE LA FONTAINE

Jazz great Miles Davis once said, **"When you hit a wrong note, it's the next note you play that determines if it's good or bad."** So, if you are having a terrible, horrible day, have hit a sinkhole of rotten luck or a day full of Murphy's luck, just play that next lucky note.

> The Comeback May Be Stronger
> Than the Setback

A LUCKY BET

Today, think about this while you are eating breakfast, perhaps eggs and ham. In 1960, two men made a bet. The wager was fifty dollars, approximately 414 in today's dollars. Not a huge amount of money, but millions of children would feel the impact. Publisher Bennett Cerf made the bet with Theodor Geisel, whom you likely know as Dr. Seuss. The challenge was that Dr. Seuss would not be able to write a successful, entertaining children's book using only fifty different words. Dr. Seuss took the bet and won. The book is Dr. Seuss's most popular title and one of the best-selling children's books in history, *Green Eggs and Ham*.

Success was not a sure thing for Theodor Geisel. He actually received his doctorate by dropping out of graduate school. Dr. Seuss was studying literature but realized he wanted to be a cartoonist, thereby dropping out of school. He later received several honorary doctorates.

No one wanted to publish Theodor Geisel's first book. Depending on the version told, anywhere from twenty to twenty-nine publishers rejected Dr. Seuss' first book, *Mulberry Street*. As he liked to tell the story, Dr. Seuss was walking down Madison Avenue, about to toss away his manuscript, when he ran into a former classmate named Mike McClintock. Mike had just been appointed junior editor of Vanguard Press. McClintock took Dr. Seuss up to his offices on Madison Avenue where Dr. Seuss signed a contract for Mulberry Street. To quote Theodor Seuss Geisel,

That's one of the reasons I believe in luck. If I'd been going down the other side of Madison Avenue, I would be in the dry- cleaning business today! [12]

LUCKY LEARNING

- » Bad luck? Don't despair. Look for the good in the bad.
- » Persist through bad luck so you are prepared when the good luck comes.
- » A positive mindset plays a large part in our success. Develop a problem-solving mindset.
- » View bad luck as a chance to grow.
- » Reframe how you react to adverse events.

Section Three

EARTH LUCK
FENG SHUI

CHAPTER 12

EARTH LUCK FENG SHUI- A LUCKY SECRET?

Remember those habits of the rich and famous? Do you want to have something else in common with Oprah Winfrey, Sir Richard Branson, Deepak Chopra, and Madonna? Steven Spielberg and Sting? They all use Feng Shui in one way or another. So, let's Free your Chi.

Bill Gates' home location, with a mountain behind it to offer protection and support, is in alignment with Feng Shui principles. This placement is in harmony with significant environmental Qi.[1]

According to ancient Feng Shui masters there are three kinds of luck: Tien, Ti, and Ren.[2]

Tien is **Heaven Luck**. Heaven Luck is the luck with which we are born. It is "in our stars" or "our karma," our early life circumstances.

Ti is ***Earth Luck***. **This is the level where Feng Shui can help strengthen your luck**. By using Feng Shui, you can create a more peaceful, energetic environment that encourages and motivates you in your day to day living.

Ren is ***Mankind Luck***. This is the luck you create with your efforts, by being prepared, by learning, by meeting the right people, by exploring the world and by growing as a human being. This is the luck we have been exploring in the above sections. You may not have realized it, but a significant portion of the book has focused on **Ren, Mankind Luck.**

In this section of the book that centers on Feng Shui, the focus will be on **Ti, Earth Luck**. We are not able to alter our **Tien, Heaven Luck.**

Feng Shui is not a religion, nor is it superstition. It is an ancient body of knowledge. For those who are ready to better their lives, Feng Shui carries a wealth of wisdom.[3]

I became interested in Feng Shui about ten years ago when my sister-in-law invited me to attend a one-session Feng Shui course with her. Later I went home, decluttered a bit and changed a few things around. At that time I was extremely busy; life got in the way and that was the end of that. A few years later the same sister-in-law and I happened to walk by a poster advertising Feng Shui classes, for which we promptly signed up, and did my life change! Serendipity? Good luck? Who knows? What I do know is that one of the most adventurous periods of my life followed. This is the course mentioned in Chapter 1, the stepping stone to taking my life in a new direction. I received wonderful employment offers, I traveled, volunteered in remote areas and encountered delightful people all over the world.

There are different types of Feng Shui; however, they are mainly different expressions of the same function, and form follows the function. There are various approaches to Feng Shui. Different approaches have somewhat varied schools of thought. It is not within the range nor the purpose of this book to deliver Feng Shui training. Learning more about Feng Shui and how it can help you is something that can be easily done via an internet search, by reading the many excellent books that are out there- with helpful photos and graphics. You can also do as I did and register for a local course and change your life. Maybe even write a book! Since the purpose of this book is to help you create more luck and not to pass an exam on Feng Shui, I am going to keep it straightforward and use the Western approach.

Feng Shui may not make you rich overnight or cure all your trials and tribulations, but you can improve the energies that influence your life.

There is much written today about decluttering, and it supports the movement towards minimalism. There are blogs and podcasts dedicated to decluttering. There are bestselling books on the art of decluttering. The very base principle of Feng Shui is that clutter has a negative effect on your energy levels. Most of us would agree with this, that an untidy, chaotic space makes it difficult to find what we need. An unkempt cluttered area may also make it difficult to concentrate.

Marelisa, of the blog daringtolivefully.com[4] wisely suggests that decluttering makes you aware that you own many more things than you need. Marelisa advocates decluttering by looking for twenty-seven items to donate or give away. In the Feng Shui philosophical system twenty-seven is a lucky number. Nine is also a Feng Shui lucky number. If both decluttering and twenty-seven overwhelm you, try removing three items for nine days.

Let's start energizing your Feng Shui to improve your luck in the areas of prosperity and wealth.

To grow our luck, the most critical areas in our home are Wealth and Prosperity or Money Corner, plus the Career, Fame and Reputation and Travel sectors.

Want a Job You Love? Let's Use a Feng Shui Assist.

Want to kick-start your employment? Perhaps you want to give your job a boost. Let's find the Career area and uplift your profession. Go to the entrance of your home you use most frequently. If you live in a condo or an apartment, you may already be lucky and only have one entry. This will be the area focused on career. Do this on a day when you are not rushed or in a hurry to go somewhere. Make an aromatic cup of tea or a soothing beverage of your choice. Perhaps that beverage will need to be a tad stronger as you go along. Take a good look around that entrance. What do you see? Old junk mail? A pile of stinky workout shoes? Hats and scarves from last winter and it is now summer?

As suggested in the blog thedeliciousday.com[5] *"Clear, Clean and De-Clutter that Area as if Your Livelihood Depends on it. Because it Does."* Are you having that stronger beverage now?

Do you recognize a theme? Declutter, declutter, declutter. Since Chi is your life or energy flow, you want to make sure nothing is blocking it. Remove outdated magazines, sort through the collection bowl of pens and clips and odds and ends, discard the outgrown children's shoes. Return those library books sitting on the shelf.

Pretend your mother-in-law is coming over for a visit. Scrape the cobwebs out of the corners. Wipe down the baseboards. Take away the cat's water dish.

Don't forget the jammed hooks and items crammed behind the door. Don't block your Chi at the entrance. As thedeliciousday.com cautions, Dead Chi = Dead End Job. Keep your main entry area clean, fresh and flowing.

Remember the Feng-Shui Career Area extends outside your front door. You are welcoming a new career, new clients or new ideas. Sweep away dead and de-composting plants and last fall's leaves. Leave nothing dead and deteriorating that might represent your career.

Make the sidewalk and doorway to your home approachable and inviting. The idea here is to make the flow of energy to the entrance very smooth, resembling flowing water. If you are in a house and can redesign your sidewalk or pathway, try to gently curve or meander the walk on its way to the door. Place gentle, bubbling water fountains along the path. Never place a water feature on either side of your front door as it produces negative energy.

> "The art of Feng Shui is to create a harmonious environment; hence using appropriate symbolisms helps in empowering our needs and desires to make it happen faster." [6]

If you live in an apartment, you will need to find a way to make the Chi in your Career area happy. In the Classic School of Feng-Shui, this will be in the North area. Feng-Shui literally means wind and water. Chi, like many of us, is delighted by water. Water features bring the energy of water into your home and water is a symbol of wealth and prosperity. Your Career area could hold pleasing water features such as a fountain, shells, boats or photos or paintings of water. Art pieces showing waterfalls are always captivating. Be sure the water depicted is flowing towards the house and not away from it.

TIPS FOR THE WORKPLACE

For a Private Office:

1. Sit with a solid wall behind you.

2. Never sit with your back to the door.

3. Sit in the most powerful spot in the office, which is the corner diagonal to the door.

4. Soften sharp corners with potted plants or draperies; however, do not use sharp plants such as cactus, as they kill energy.

5. Place tables and chairs in a way that allows energy to flow. Furniture should not block the flow of chi.

For the Main Office:

6. Employees should not be seated facing one another, which may be seen as confrontational.

7. If there are cubicles, try to have each employee, sit with a 'wall' behind them.

8. A water arrangement in the front of the office encourages money coming in. Ensure that the water is flowing inwards to the office.

9. Plants are beneficial to the office as they represent growth luck. Therefore, they are a boon to the office. Place plants in the east or southeast direction. Just remember not to use plants with pointed leaves or sharp bits such as cacti.

YOUR WEALTH AND MONEY AREA

Looking for **luck** in all the wrong places? Let's make sure you look in your Wealth and Money Area. In Western Feng Shui, this will be in the upper left area of your home. In classical Feng Shui, this will be in the Southeast area.

Can money grow on trees? Not likely. But your luck can. Have you ever heard of a Lucky Bamboo plant? Chances are you have. It is even more likely that you have seen one in your local florist or garden center. Lucky Bamboo plants have become more and more popular in recent years, and there is a good reason why. You will love your Wealth Area as this is where money grows on trees! The interplay of Wood, Water, and Earth elements is essential in the décor and arrangement of your Wealth and Money Area. Create a mini indoor garden area full of lush, green, healthy plants such as a **lucky bamboo plant**. You can find a "lucky" bamboo plant in most floral shops or stores nowadays.

The Spruce Reports that the lucky bamboo is considered lucky as it is an amazing plant that brings peaceful and wise energy into your home. The plant expresses all five Feng Shui elements: Water, Wood, Fire, Earth, and Metal. Rocks placed in the pot represent the earth. A red ribbon that is usually tied to the plant represents fire. Lastly, the plant will be potted in a metal container or have a metal coin for Good Luck. There may also be a metal figurine, such as the Laughing Buddha.

The number of stalks has a specific meaning you will want to take into consideration to increase your luck in certain areas:[7,8]

2 for *Love and Marriage, Abundance and Double the Luck Factor*

3 for *Happiness, Long Life and Career Promotions*

5 for *Positive Health Energy*

6 for *Opportunities to Increase Wealth*

8 for *Wealth and Abundance*

9 for *Good Fortune*

10 for *Giving a person a perfect, happy life-denotes all things good in life*

Be sure to take good care of your lucky plant. Rodika Tchi, of thespruce.com, relates that you don't want the only luck to be the "lucky to be alive" factor.[7] Be sure to cultivate your plant and your good luck.

MORE TIPS FOR YOUR WEALTH AND MONEY AREA

As in your Career area, you can decorate with water features such real fountains or images of water. Be sure the water is clean and flowing and not stagnant. Mirrors are helpful in this area, too.

Highlight particular shapes in your Money Area. Each element is expressed in specific forms. You can incorporate the desired element with shapes such as:

- » Rectangular- Wood Element
- » Square- Earth Element
- » Wavy- Water Element

Integrate these shapes through picture frames, fabric patterns, wallpaper, and art. The Wood element is smoothly blended through the use of your Lucky Bamboo or images of forests, parks or natural landscapes.

A unique touch is to include images that represent, to you, visions of wealth and abundance. These might be people enjoying a vacation on a sandy beach, a waterfront house, a family gathered around a table laden with delicious foods, a new baby or a university diploma.

Don't shell out extra money for luck. Just shell out. Every year thousands of tourists collect or buy seashells while visiting the seashore. Shells conjure images of peaceful, stress-free days at tropical beaches.

Conch shells and cowrie shells are said to augment travel luck.

> Feng Shui tenets say that shells are useful to attract overseas business and relationship luck. They are also an excellent symbol for those who wish to have a harmonious relationship with the rich and the famous.[9]

A lovely, large shell of at least 6-8 inches placed at the South sector of the living room, enhances the good reputation and name of the occupant. Shells situated in the southwest or the Northeast sectors of the living room strengthen education and relationship luck.

HEALTHY LUCK

Traditionally, Feng Shui is more than a matter of luck. It is about living harmoniously with the natural world. Chi, the universal energy that permeates everything, is constantly on the move. For health, in particular, smooth flowing chi is everything.

To activate excellent health luck, you can place items suggestive of trees, in the East of any room. These features might include the following:

- » A healthy plant.
- » Any object made of wood.
- » A decorative dragon carved of wood or made of china.

- » Any object that symbolizes both wood and water.
- » Pictures of healthy, young looking flowers or plants.

> "With good Feng Shui, health can improve, opportunities to make money can increase, and career prospects can improve—but the individual must still seize these opportunities through his or her efforts." [10]

Section Five

LUCKY CHARMERS
LUCKY CHARMS
LUCKY TRAVEL
HAPPY GO LUCKY

CHAPTER 13

LUCKY CHARMERS

> I don't see myself as extremely handsome. I just figure I can charm you into liking me.
>
> WESLEY SNIPES

The door opened. A new person arrived at the gathering. Average, nice looking, but not a magazine model. A quick smile, a lift of the brow, and the individual slipped gracefully into the group, immediately absorbed into the lively conversation. All the while you still stood against the wall, wondering what this person had that you didn't. What made this lucky individual so easily likeable? Is charm just some mysterious X-factor that some people are born with, and other unlucky people lack?

Luckily for us, scientists have been hard at work on this question. Being likeable and alluring is a matter of emotional intelligence. We can learn to be charming.

Whether you want to be lucky in love or lucky in work, a first-impression counts. An excellent premier impression is all about body language. Smile with your eyes, as well as your mouth. A charming smile is one where you use your entire face to smile. Make your light shine through.

There are forty-three muscles in the face. Use them well. As in the old song lyric, when you are smiling the whole world smiles with you. Research has shown that people make judgements about someone's competence, trustworthiness, and likeability after seeing their face for less than a tenth of a second. Professor Alexander Todorov[1], a psychology professor at Princeton, states that things like trustworthiness and attractiveness are highly dependent on facial expressions. So put on a happy face. Slap on a lucky grin. Let's face it. While you are born with the face you've got, you can alter your expression by smiling. Todorov explains that people discern a smiling face as warm, trustworthy, and sociable.

You can train yourself to be charming. Who could better educate us in body language than an FBI agent? Jack Schafer is a likeability coach and the author of The Like Switch.[2] Schafer suggests that there are three physical gestures we do that indicate we are not a threat. When we approach someone, to show friendliness, we perform a quick eyebrow flash-an up and down movement which lasts about a sixth of a second, carry out a slight head tilt, and we smile.

Make other people feel good about themselves. Focus on the other person. In North America, eye contact signifies sincerity. Be aware that in different cultures, you could bring bad luck upon yourself as prolonged eye contact can signify hostility or aggressiveness.

While it is true about first impressions-that you never get a second chance to make them-you do get a chance for a do-over or to create a second chance at luck. Third and fourth chances for that matter. What else can you do to increase your odds of being found charming? How do you become the sort of person everyone wants to talk to? Whether you are at a networking event, meeting clients, or trying to make new friends, being able to win people over is an important competency.

YOUR CHARM CHECKLIST

- ✓ Put on a happy face. Smile.
- ✓ Portray perfect posture. Head high, shoulders back, back straight. Strong stance is a success barometer. Sturdy posture implies power. Many leading men are shorter than we think. Tom Cruise is 5 feet 7 inches tall (172 cm). Daniel Radcliffe is 5 feet 5 inches tall (165 cm). Robin Williams was 5 feet 7 inches tall (172 cm). Bruno Mars is 5 feet 5 inches tall (165 cm.).
- ✓ Become the kind of person who is interested in other people. We all love an opportunity to talk about ourselves. Ensure the conversation revolves around the other person – ask questions, remember to smile, and make eye contact. Be entirely focused on the person with whom you are conversing.
- ✓ Remember people's names and use them. Learn a simple memory technique to remember names. When you first meet someone, repeat their name to memorize it and then occasionally drop it into the conversation.
- ✓ Speak the correct body language. Ensure your arms are open and not crossed. Mirror your conversation partner's

mannerisms, including tone of voice and style. Use words they use.

- ✓ Be a good listener. Actively listen. Smile and nod. Use non-words such as uh-huh and uh-hum. These are good indicators that you are listening. Put your phone down and turn to face your partner, pointing your shoulders and torso in his or her direction. Focus on what your partner is saying. Did they say something that you might want to explore? Ask them how their week went. Ask questions that move the topic forward.
- ✓ Look for "Latch" words. In other words, look for interests you both share. Search for common ground. As the other person is speaking, listen for words that fit your interests, words onto which you can "latch." When your conversation partner is finished speaking, you can use these words to segue into more conversation through questions. You can develop an emotional connection.
- ✓ Are you going to a significant meet and greet? Maybe you have a sales call, an information meeting, a negotiation or a get to know you lunch. You want the other person to be charmed by you and to take you seriously from the start. Make that happen with one simple email. Send a pre-meeting email. This email confirms the meeting, reminds them who you are and why you are meeting. It establishes your credentials without you having to brag about them and hopefully, gets the other person excited to meet you.[3]

The article, 13 Habits of Exceptionally Likable People,[4] reinforces and adds to the above suggestions. The research shared in the article strengthens the arguments for creating a strong first impression, using positive body language, remembering and using people's names, putting away your phones, and asking questions of others.

Additional **Charisma Creators** include:

Be genuine. People gravitate to others they can trust. Likeable people are sincere and honest; they are comfortable in their skin. Authentic people do what makes them happy-not what they think will make others like them.

Be open-minded. Being open-minded makes a person approachable. People do not want to talk to someone who has a closed mind, someone who has already formed an opinion and is not willing to listen. Make an effort to understand others. Be empathetic.

Don't be the Attention Seeker. People are contemptuous of those who repeatedly have to be the center of attention. Being a loud extrovert is not always necessary. Being friendly, confident and attentive can make you more likeable.

Be thankful. Two adjectives that are closely tied to likeability are *appreciative* and *humble*. Pay attention to others who have helped you. We all need help along the way. Be grateful.

Be consistent. Feeling grumpy, crabby, irritable or bad-tempered? We have all been there, but try to be consistent and reliable. People want to know that when they approach you, they will be approaching Dr. Jeykll, not Mr. Hyde.

The article mentioned above notes a study conducted at UCLA in which participants rated adjectives according to their perceived significance to likeability. Surprisingly the top-rated attributes were not those associated with innate characteristics such as intelligence or attractiveness. Instead, the highest rated adjectives were transparency, sincerity, and capacity for understanding another person.

CHAPTER 14

LUCKY CHARMS

As a child, do you remember gobbling down your **Lucky cereal** and then running out to play? If you are old enough, and lucky enough (especially if you have siblings), perhaps you also have fun memories of digging down into the cereal box for that toy or lucky charm. Oh, your mother probably tried to make you do it in a sanitary way by slowly pouring the cereal into a bowl until that magic prize appeared. But you were much too excited and eager to wait.

As adults, we still use our lucky charms. Go to any casino or bingo hall to see proof.

Good luck symbols have existed just about as long as humankind. Lucky charms are common in every culture worldwide. Many people pass them off as mere superstition. Others have faith and say charms of chance work. Maybe these tokens of fortune do seem effective because our attitude and behavior change according to what we believe. It could be our thoughts and the action we take when we think something to be true do make things happen accordingly.

THE THINGS WE DO FOR LUCK

Not a positive Pollyanna? You might want to be more charming. Research has shown you can become more confident by using a lucky charm. During a study conducted at the University of Cologne in Germany in 2010, superstitious subjects were asked to play a memory game; people allowed to use their talismans while they played scored higher than those who played without their amulets.[1]

In an article reported by Popular Science[2], researchers told one set of golfers they were golfing with a "lucky" ball. The researchers told another set of golfers that they were golfing with the same ball everyone else had used. The golfers with "lucky" balls performed significantly better.

Test subjects allowed to hold onto their "lucky-charms" from home while solving an anagram puzzle performed better. The theory is that people allowed to use their "lucky-charms" persisted at problems longer because they felt more effective, perhaps having the assistance of some other power.[3]

Activating luck-related superstitions through a common saying or action (e.g., break a leg or crossing your fingers) or using a lucky charm improves ensuing performance in anagram games, memory, golf and motor dexterity. Researchers felt the benefits resulted from changes in perceived self-efficacy.

Initiating a superstition heightens users' confidence in forthcoming undertakings, which in turn, improves performance.[4]

Participating in harmless rituals makes us feel better when we're nervous. These include wearing a lucky jersey (or special underwear), rubbing a lucky penny, and knocking on wood. We often use these gestures in high anxiety situations to help reduce anxiety and make us feel we have some control over the situation. We feel less anxious and perform better.[5]

New research shows gestures that involve pushing away from the body, such as throwing salt, spitting, or knocking on wood, are effective for helping people feel protected from adverse outcomes. These are especially effective in situations where people are trying to undo bad luck.

If you are a North American hockey fan you know all about those playoff beards! For the uninitiated, this is a Stanley Cup playoff superstition. During playoff season NHL players do not shave. This is a superstition said to bring good luck. It is not so much about looking intimidating with a burly beard but more about not changing anything when you are on a lucky streak.

Lucky Rituals: Athletes and gamblers use these rituals because they believe they will then keep on winning. **Touch wood.**

Lucky Charms to Charm You

In many western cultures, charms are not only a symbol of good luck, but they have also become a symbol of individuality. Historically, charms have been a symbol of luck, protection or a status symbol. Today people wear charms on bracelets, anklets, necklaces, shoes, and pins as ways to demonstrate accomplishments or indicate personal likes. Sharing the same charm is a way to show a connection.

Leafy Luck: You have likely been living under a toadstool if you haven't heard about lucky **four-leaf clovers** as an ancient Irish symbol of luck. But do you know why they are supposed to be lucky? The four leaves were thought to have the mystical powers of faith, hope, love and luck. If you have been out digging in your garden for some lucky clover you may have pushed your luck. True four-leaf clovers are rare, with only one in 10,000 plants carrying the lucky leaves. The lucky ones come from the white clover plant called Trifolium repens.[6]

> Remember not to iron your four-leaf clover.
> If you do, you will be pressing your luck.

The Lucky Horseshoe: Horseshoes are thought to bring luck and protection. You may have seen them hanging over doorways, as tattoos, or worn as jewelry. Over the centuries, several stories have emerged as to the origins of the luck of the horseshoe. There is an Irish story of the blacksmith and the devil. One day the blacksmith was toiling hard in his shop, forging horseshoes. The devil appeared and demanded his own shoes. The blacksmith took burning hot shoes and nailed them into the devil's hooves. The devil, in excruciating pain, tore off the shoes and swore he would never go near horseshoes again. Thus, the tradition of hanging horseshoes over entrances to ward off evil spirits began.

Western Europeans believed iron had magical powers; iron could drive away evil. Horseshoes, made of iron, kept away the malevolent fairies.

Even the number of holes in a horseshoe is considered lucky. Lucky seven!

Hanging a horseshoe heels up prevents the luck from running out; hanging a horseshoe heels down means it flows good luck on everyone who walks beneath it. Perhaps it wouldn't hurt to have two and hang one each way! [7]

> The Lucky Horseshoe-May It Bring Luck, Love
> and Happiness to All Who Share It.

Luck Be a Lady Tonight: Or maybe a **Ladybug**. In many cultures, ladybugs are thought to bring luck. Some cultures think that if a ladybug lands on you and you don't brush it off, your luck will improve. However, not all ladybugs are created equal. The deeper the red color and the more spots a bug has, the luckier you will be. Looking to fall in love or get married? In Belgium, a ladybug crawling across a maiden's hand was a sign she would soon be married. Need a groom? If a man and a woman see a ladybug at the same time, they will fall in love. If you want to remain healthy, don't kill that bug! Killing a ladybug can bring you misfortune.

Acorns: According to a Norse superstition, placing an acorn on a windowsill will protect a house from being struck by lightning. For more luck, you can use blind pulls shaped like acorns.

When Pigs Fly: The pig is a symbol of prosperity, fertility and lots of good luck. Swine farmers were always known to have food. Keeping pigs was a sure way of ensuring your family's well-being.

Pigs are associated with wealth. Many lucky people wear small pig charms to attract money and good luck. Pigs have a history of ensuring a family's finances. Pig charms remain popular to this day. Did you ever wonder why, as children, we put our money in a piggy bank? Feeding our piggy bank with coins is a sure sign that we are caring for our financial future. Piggy banks are thought to protect and attract money.

Candy in shapes of pigs symbolizes wishes of prosperity and luck. Every December, in Northern Europe, marzipan pigs are sold in the thousands. In Norwegian, the term "heldiggris" literally translates to "lucky pig."

CHAPTER 15

LUCKY TRAVEL

> He who does not venture has no luck.
>
> Proverb

Go. Travel. Travel by plane. Travel by ship, by foot or in a car. Travel in a book, in your head, close to home or afar. But travel you must.

For many people, being able to travel the world is a dream. People who have voyaged frequently are seen as lucky. Is it pure happenstance or are these **lucky** travelers creating wonderful opportunities?

You will not know your luck until you travel. I know, you are saying, "Not everyone can travel. Nor does everyone want to." But you should. Want to, that is. Go. See. See your luck. Lie on a Caribbean cerulean beach, on a dusty African plain or near an Asian holy temple. Open your eyes at night. Count your lucky stars.

Don't just sit on the runway of life wishing for luck. Many travel naysayers imagine what is holding them back is lack of money. They believe people who get to travel are lucky or special. These same people are likely the people who don't make it to the gym or have excuses why they can't get a good job or achieve something else they desire. They have not yet developed their **lucky mindset.**

> Travel is more than the seeing of sights;
> it is a change that goes on, deep and
> permanent, in the ideas of living.
> MIRIAM BEARD

If you recall from chapter 4, lucky people are open to new opportunities and embrace uncertainty.

Traveling promotes neurogenesis, which is the growth and development of neurons. Paul Nussbaum[1], a neuropsychologist from the University of Pittsburgh argues that traveling promotes neurogenesis. Travel allows our brain to experience novel and complex environments. These new challenges cause the brain to propagate dendrites.

Only have time for a weekend getaway? You don't need to travel the world to reap these benefits. A weekend road trip to an unfamiliar city gives your brain the same stimulation.

> Not All Those Who Wander Are Lost
> J.R. TOLKIEN, LORD OF THE RINGS

Let travel present you with the numerous opportunities that await you. Here are a few:

- » **You practice and improve your communication skills.** Your new competence may include learning some language basics of the country you are visiting, learning about body language and learning some of the country's cultural values in order not to offend your hosts. For example, in some countries, it is rude to make direct eye contact or extend your left hand.

- » **You develop organization and planning skills.** Planning multi-stop, multi-city/county trips is a lot of work. It takes much planning, either advanced or along the way. What modes of transportation will you use? Where will you stay? What is most cost-effective? Are you planning for just yourself or a group? A bonus is that you may have an additional skill for your resume, particularly if you coordinated travel for a group.

- » **You broaden your horizons.** You meet people from a variety of cultures and along the way see life from different angles. You adopt a global view of the world and start to see how interconnected we are as humans, which helps reduce prejudice and narrow-mindedness.

- » **You boost your confidence.** You learn to overcome obstacles and handle unplanned situations.

- » **You learn the world is your classroom.** You increase your knowledge of geography, languages, and cultures.

- » **You improve your job performance and increase creativity.**[2] Vacations help us recharge and reconnect with ourselves. Holidays assist with enhancing the quality of life, which in turn can lead to an increased caliber of work on the job.

- » **You boost your happiness, not only by traveling, but from just planning a trip.** A Cornell University study reports the anticipation of taking a vacation is far greater than the anticipation of acquiring a physical possession.[3]

- » **You appreciate your friends and family.** When we travel, we often have time to reflect-often upon the things we take for granted. Sometimes this includes our friends and family.

- » **You become more adaptable.** Indeed, travel is one way to learn to become more flexible and to turn what might be seen as bad luck into good luck. Flight delayed? See it as a chance to read your new book, chat with interesting people, or if the delay is exceptionally long, explore a different city.

TURN YOUR TRAVELS INTO A RESUME BUILDER AND MARKETABLE JOB SKILLS

Here are some employment skill takeaway-resume builders:

You developed excellent communication skills-the ability to overcome language and cultural barriers. Perhaps you can now converse in French, Spanish, or Korean.

You are adaptable and able to change plans as necessary and can handle issues quickly and calmly.

Maybe you developed invaluable budget and planning skills, including devising, saving, monitoring and analyzing financial risk.

Did you blog, post or create other travel publications? Perhaps you created, launched and hosted a website. Feasibly, you contributed travel articles to lifestyle websites and blogs.

Possibly, you governed and monitored online traffic and social media.

In interviews, use travel stories to illustrate skills which make you a memorable candidate.

TAKE YOUR LUCK TO HEART

How lucky is this! Traveling keeps us healthier. In a big way. Want to reduce your chances of having a heart attack? Take a vacation. According to a joint study from the Global Commission on Aging and the Transamerica Center for Retirement Studies in partnership with the U.S. Travel Association, women who take two vacations a year significantly lower their risk of suffering a heart attack as compared to those who only travel every six years. Males who do not take an annual vacation have a twenty percent higher risk of death. Men who don't vacation also have a thirty percent greater risk of heart disease.[4]

Despite the negative reviews we can sometimes hear about the dangers of travel; scientific studies still show that travel reduces stress. Travelers report feeling less anxious and are in a better mood than they were before their holiday. These feelings linger for weeks.

Travel has many other blessings. It gives you new insights, new ways of seeing the world. People often discover a fresh sense of purpose and direction.

You also realize that money can't buy happiness. Yes, we need a certain amount of money to have our needs met. But often we put so much emphasis on climbing the career ladder that we forget to climb the mountains of joy the world has to offer. Traveling helps us see that life isn't only about money. It gives us fresh eyes on the magic of the world, delights that we become immune to in our backyard.

> Twenty years from now you will be more disappointed by the things you that didn't do than by the ones you did do. So throw off the bowlines. Sail away from the safe harbor. Catch the trade winds in your sails. Explore. Dream. Discover.
> **MARK TWAIN**

The key is to take the first step. All-inclusive resorts and short-term cruises are delightful if you only have a week of holidays and you need a quick, easy, stress-free getaway. However, if you are at all able, take a more extended trip. Be open to all kinds of delightful, serendipitous experiences.

You might think that finding luck is hard or that it is hiding in a bush somewhere, but that is not the case. Until it is.

One of my fondest, most amusing travel stories happened during five days in San Francisco. My husband and I were walking down the street in the Fisherman's Wharf area, totally immersed in enjoying the sights and sounds. All at once a full, leafy bush jumped from the boulevard to land smack dab in front of us. Naturally, I screamed and jumped about five feet into the air. The milling crowd on the sidewalk around us whooped and chortled and then burst into applause. What on earth was going on? A lithe, shoeless little man in tattered clothes emerged from the bush, whipped off his hat and passed it around to the enthralled audience. The sidewalk crowd delighted in watching the bushman startle his next unsuspecting victim. As part of the entertainment, I did not see the need to pay! However, I did stick around to watch the next show. This man's bush routine was repeated over and over again with the same reaction from the crowd. They loved it. And they opened their wallets.

Here was a man making his luck. From his lack of shoes and tattered clothing, one would surmise that he was down on his luck. However, he made the most of what he had. A bush! Plus, a new audience every hour, every day. Bushman was definitely taking advantage of Opportunity Luck and creating his own karma.

Luck is tenacity of purpose.

ELBERT HUBBARD

For many, travel is not within their circumstances at the moment. Those of us who do get to travel are fortunate.

Can't afford to travel? Don't have the vacation time to travel? Family constraints holding you back? Travel to your library. We are so lucky to have access to the riches of libraries. Travel through books. One can learn wildly wonderful things about the world, both through National Geographic travel type books and even through fiction.

> Just go. Go. Go! I don't care how.
> You can go by foot. You can go by cow.
> Kid, you'll move mountains! Today is your day!
> Your mountain is waiting. So get on your way! –
> Oh, The Places You Will Go!
>
> **DR. SEUSS**

Many people with office jobs and limited holidays feel they don't have time to travel as much as they would like to. Nomadic Matt[5] advocates that many people have more time to journey than they think they do. Matt argues that if you count two weeks' vacation time plus weekends, you can travel up to 110 days per year. Matt suggests spending a weekend away somewhere. A weekend is enough time to explore a bustling city, wander through a quaint town or explore a national park.

If you live in a large city, travel to a different part of town; one you have never explored. Be a tourist in your borough. Discover all the touristy spots, the ones to which the locals never go.

Nomadic Matt recommends leaving your house and staying elsewhere. Otherwise, it will be too tempting to do housework or run errands. It is essential to break your routine so that you feel more like you have had a bit of a holiday.

Exploring your city could mean exploring your limitations and fears. If you've lived in your town for a long time, or always, your world can become reduced to a small radius of favorite spaces and places-so that you forget to look further afield. Explore a side of the city you have never seen before. Who knows what luck you will encounter there. A romantic partner? A new hobby? A new group of friends? Your new favorite place to hang?

> A wise traveler never despises his own country.
> CARLO GOLDONI

Increase your chances on taking a chance by:

- » Signing up for an event.
- » Paying ahead of time so it is harder to back out.
- » Invite a buddy-an associative habit.
- » Joining a Meetup group via the Meetup app.
- » Volunteering-Remember all those benefits from volunteering!
- » Learning a new craft, hands-on skill or language in a new area of the city.

Your comfort zone is greater than 4 kilometers. A few years ago my husband and I were lucky enough to visit relatives living in Bermuda, a series of islands totaling 53.3 kilometers or 20.6 square miles. The main island, which is the one often referred to as Bermuda is 22.5 kilometers or fourteen miles long. We were staying in the area of St. George's. One day we took the bus to Hamilton, the capital of Bermuda, a distance of four kilometers from our accommodation. Put that number in your head; four kilometers or approximately 2.5 miles. On the return trip, by bus, to St. George, a friendly, local gentleman began to chat with us. For about fifteen minutes of the forty-five minute ride, Jack regaled us with town tales and regional history. Just before his stop, Jack asked us where we were staying. When we replied, "St. George's" Jack looked at us in awe and retorted, "Wow, that's far. I was born there. I haven't been there in fifteen years." Jack then promptly stepped off the bus. I think my jaw stayed open for five minutes. My mind kept repeating, "Just stay on the bus, Jack."

In fifteen years, Jack had not traveled more than two kilometers, not even to go to St. George's where he was born. Perhaps he had no reason to. But wouldn't curiosity send him there? Don't we all drive by the house where we grew up just to reflect and think about our childhood? Had the tiny size of the island so restricted Jack's sense of size and space that two more kilometers felt huge to him? The point here is not to let yourself become so accustomed to your space that you no longer venture beyond it.

BE PREPARED: As noted earlier, lucky people are not only willing to venture, they are also prepared. Do your research. Know not only where you are staying and how you are getting there, but also read travel advice columns. Try to learn at least the basics of the local language. Being able to say please and thank you goes a long way. If you are going to be away for any length of time, learn key phrases and 'taxi language.'

1. Stop here. Turn here.
2. Where is _____ ?
3. How far away is _____ ?
4. How much does it cost to go to _____?
5. Where is the café/restaurant?

Also, learn café/restaurant language. Learn the names of the basic foods and drink and learn how to order them.

Travel with the right attitude. To enjoy **lucky** trips, try the following suggestions:

Keep an open mind. Live the culture you are experiencing. Remember serendipity and the trait of being aware of opportunities.

> If you reject the food, ignore the customs,
> fear the religion and avoid the people,
> you might better stay at home.
> JAMES MICHENER

Don't use fear as an excuse to avoid adventure. Lucky travelers don't fall victim to crime due to their ignorance. Instead, they avert scams and become street-wise. Become a chameleon. Blending in may not be physically possible, but you can mingle clothing wise. Purchase a few local garments and wear them. You won't look so newly arrived.

As you are preparing for your trip and packing your bag, here are some ways you can pack some travel luck:

- » The conch shell is often called the traveler's shell. It is particularly forceful for those traveling for business. Place a conch or cowrie shell in your suitcase promising energy. The conch is known for smooth, uninterrupted travel, business rewards, and excellent communication during business meetings. The cowrie is a suitable stand-in for the conch shell. Do be careful of article restriction laws if traveling internationally.

- » For love in travels: Carry any quartz, especially rose quartz jewelry or a lucky charm on your person or pack some in your suitcase.

- » Travel to another country (travel across water) brings good luck.

> I travel not to go anywhere, but to go.
> I travel for travel's sake.
> ROBERT LOUIS STEVENSON

CHAPTER 16

HAPPY GO LUCKY HAPPY LUCK

Here is an intriguing fact. The words luck and happiness are cognates, which means the words have the same ancestral root. They are related. This is true for every Indo-European language, all the way back to ancient Greek. The connection between the two words suggests that for many ancient peoples—and for many others long after that, happiness was not something you could control.[1] Today, a lot of people still assume that being happy means you are fortunate, that you have a blessed, lucky, life.

As in the expression happy go lucky, it seems happiness and luck go hand in hand. Here are a few suggestions for increasing your joy.

Control your happiness. Wondering what's been reported to be the number one contributor to happiness? Money? Good Looks? Sex? The answer is none of these. According to a report by *The Journal of Personality and Social Psychology*, the answer is *'autonomy'* - defined as *"the feeling that your life - its activities and habits -- are self-chosen and self-endorsed."* [2]

Psychologists suggest taking back your happiness by tapping into your internal locus of control. Create a disciplined schedule. Stop sleeping late and watching too much T.V. Pre-set deadlines and do things in a timely, efficient manner. Establish a daily routine with goals. Research shows that goals make you happier.[3]

Hello. This tip seems counterintuitive, but listening to sad music on repeat apparently makes us happy. Listening to blue music creates peacefulness and positive feelings in the listener. Most of us have experienced the therapeutic effects of a good cry. Listening to sad music can boost our mood.[4]

Spend your money on experiences rather than more possessions. According to psychological research, experiences, through memories, continue to provide happiness long after the event occurred. People reported a greater sense of "being alive" during experiences.[5]

A purrrfect way to get happy. Cuddle with your cat, canoodle with your canine. Pets can provide meaningful social support. If you want to be more outgoing, less lonely, and become more fit, get a pet. In a study reported in Psychology Today, dog owners reported feeling happier and healthier. It makes me happy to know there was no support for the 'crazy cat lady' hypothesis![6]

Buy Time-Not Things. Money cannot buy happiness; how you spend it can. According to a study titled *Proceedings of the National Academy of Sciences*[7], people are happier when they spend money on time-saving services such as lawn care, grocery delivery, and house cleaning. In comparison, money spent on material purchases was less likely to elicit positive emotions. The reason may be that investing in time-saving services reduces the stress of daily chores and allows people more time to spend on pleasurable activities.

It's All About the Sweat. Focus more on what's important to you and don't sweat the small stuff. Let go of toxic relationships and past failures. But do sweat. Exercise. Happiness and exercise work together in a continuous cycle. "Exercise increases the production of brain chemicals that help alleviate pain and boost feelings of euphoria. And if you feel happy, you are more likely to exercise." [8] A single workout can have immediate effects on your brain; it will increase levels of dopamine, serotonin, and noradrenaline, thus improving your mood right after your workout. If you become a long-term exerciser, you receive long-lasting increases in the good mood neurotransmitters.

Savor this. Do what the happiest people in the world do. The next time something good happens, stop and appreciate the moment. As in the old cliché, stop and smell the roses. The happiness experts call this **savoring**. Most of us are so busy multi-tasking, we forget to pay attention to individual things. Savoring can be as simple as appreciating your morning coffee. Smell it, taste it, enjoy it. Whatever you are doing: drinking, eating, cooking, bathing, chatting with a loved one, do one thing at a time and don't hurry through it.

As many of us intuitively know, walks in nature decrease stress and increase well-being. According to an article in wilderness.org[9], short, frequent hikes are more beneficial than long, occasional ones. Go for a walk. Not just any walk-a Savoring Walk. Observe the sights, sounds and smells you encounter.

What plants do you see? What birds, frogs, crickets, bubbling brooks do you hear?

Go Outdoors. According to Time Magazine[10], getting outdoors is the No. 1 beneficial thing we can do daily to improve life. Spending time outdoors boosts cognition and creativity and enhances sleep. Natural environments stimulate creative play in children and encourage socialization. Spending time in natural spaces makes us happier people, which ripples outwards into our families and social groups.

Be Grateful. Keep a gratitude journal. In a study[11] on the benefits of gratitude, researchers asked participants to write in a journal. One group was asked to briefly describe five things for which they were grateful. Another group was asked to write about events that were hassles-things that displeased them. A control group was asked to simply write about events that affected them, without any positive or negative comments. The participants who wrote about being grateful reported feeling more joyful, enthusiastic, interested, attentive, energetic, excited, determined, and stronger than those in the hassles group.

Challenge Yourself. Try something new. Try something that scares you, something out of your comfort zone. Often, we know we are unhappy where we are, but the alternatives are just too scary. We prefer the devil we know even if it doesn't make us happy. Who knows, you may have a serendipitous moment, and you may find that special something that you have been searching for but haven't quite been able to identify.

Be Purpose-Oriented. Live a purposeful life. Be purpose oriented as well as goal driven. Designing a purposeful action does not have an end. It may be lifelong whereas a goal driven achievement is finite. One example is the desire to be a life-long learner. A goal might be taking a specific course or getting a degree. A purposeful desire would be continuous learning in various ways: courses, reading, watching Ted Talks, attending lectures, etc. Saving up to buy a house is an admirable goal. Continuing to be responsible with money after achieving your goal would constitute living with intention. Goals are not your final objective. Research indicates that being purpose oriented rather than money directed at work, can lead to greater success. Have a purposeful reason to show up at work each week. Another excellent reason is that living with intention creates those all-important habits we rely on.[12]

Keep a one-sentence journal. Jot down special, little moments and note who you were with. Research show how much people enjoy reliving memories of the day-to-day moments from their lives. Rereading the event months later brings us joy.[13]

Use lovely notebooks or moleskins. My husband noticed I was always jotting down notes in dollar store journals. One day at a craft market he bought me a delightful, leather bound mini journal. It was so pretty I was reluctant to mar it by actually writing in it. Now, I find happiness by using it to note book titles and ideas for future gifts that will spoil me. As lovely as this is, there is actually a scientific basis for writing in a notebook rather than recording ideas on our phones. The act of writing by hand makes us smarter. And that should make all of us happy. By picking up a pen and writing, we're more likely to process information. Using notebooks is a titan habit. Author, Tim

Ferriss,[14] is well known for the number of notebook journals he has kept for many years.

Catch Up with Friends in Unique Ways. Rather than always meeting over coffee or beer try catching up with one another in a unique place or doing an enjoyable activity. Go on long drives together, make soup and share it, build a birdhouse or something more manly, if you have the skills. Go hiking or paint your condo.

Kindness Challenge. We have all heard "engage in unique random acts of kindness." Sure, this will make us happy, but sometimes it sounds like a repeat. Why not try some unique acts of kindness? Challenge your friends. Have a contest.

Volunteer. Volunteering makes you happy. The more you give of yourself, the more joyous you will feel. Researchers measured brain activity and hormones to discover that being helpful conveys enormous pleasure.[15] The social aspect of working with and helping others also helps combat depression, relieve stress and alleviate anxiety.

Be Complimentary. Compliment someone. Giving a meaningful compliment is an invaluable way to make yourself happier. It may seem counterintuitive, but it works. Try it. You don't have to give compliments on huge matters. Focus on small items or accomplishments. That works just as well. Tell someone how great their tie, earrings, shirt, or shoes are. Mention the fact they are always positive. Like someone's smile. Compliment a barista.

List a Few of Your Favorite Things. If you love to read, keep a log of books you want to peruse. The next time you are in a bookstore or a library, you can look to your list for suggestions of books to read. Dictate your checklist on your phone, and you will always have the record with you. Of course, if you want to get smarter, as noted above, you will write your list in your new, natty, notebook. Perhaps keep an inventory of your favorite restaurants and cafes. How often does someone suggest going out to eat and then everyone goes blank as to which restaurant to recommend. How about a list of your favorite things? The next time Christmas or your birthday rolls around, and someone asks you what you would like for a gift, you can refer to your prized items list.

Have a Treat. Just not every day. If you stop at the same Starbucks for your favorite coffee or scone on a daily basis, take a break for a few days. When you do return, the coffee, muffin or delicacy that you love, is going to be even more amazing. Make it a treat. Savor it. You will also be tapping into your locus of self-control. Maybe the treat you love can be a habit reward. You will save money not buying the treat every day. Alternately, you could do a small kindness and give away your goody. All that from one small item. Aren't you lucky!

Laugh. The old cliché, *Laughter is the best medicine*, has a lot of truth to it. Humor has many benefits. Humor is beneficial for coping with stress. It helps reduce the risk of heart attack and stroke. Laughter can reduce pain during dental work. Those who use humor as a coping mechanism can live up to four and a half years longer.

> I like people who make me laugh…
> It cures a multitude of ills.
> AUDREY HEPBURN

Embrace Being Imperfect. Don't give in to the quest for perfection, which drives us to never feel good enough. Appreciate your worthiness and you will be happier.

Find Joy in Little Things.

- Start each day with a smile. *"When you're smiling the whole world smiles with you."* Research shows when you smile you trigger smile muscles in others.

- Always look behind you- for items you may have left. A backward glance is an excellent custom to help not forget belongings such as briefcases, purses, jackets, and scarves overlooked on benches or restaurant chairs. I am the queen of left behind items – but no more!

- Buy a favorite mug, glass, or bottle from which to drink. Treat yourself to some high-end coffee, tea or other drink and savor it in your special spot.

- Touch your toes. Touching your toes can increase blood flow to the brain and release stress.

- Daydream. Visualize your future. Let your mind wander. Be creative.

- Play in the dirt. A harmless bacteria found in soil has been discovered to have a similar effect on humans to antidepressants.

FENG-SHUI HAPPY LUCK
Design a Happy, Healthy Living Environment

- » **Invite in nature.** Open your doors and windows. Surround yourself with fresh air, light, and greenery. One of the tenets of ancient Feng-Shui philosophy is harmony with nature. Use plants to bring elements of nature into your home. Plants are excellent Feng-Shui as they are a wood element. They also grow upwards, representing growth.[16]

- » **Lighten Up.** A space with good Feng-Shui has good lighting and is a happy place. Open your bedroom curtains as soon as you wake in the morning. Do the same for other areas you enter in the morning such as the kitchen or home office. If you don't have enough natural light, strategically use mirrors to reflect more light.

- » **Color Choice.** Choose calming colors, colors that help you unwind. Look for soothing greens, blues, lavenders, peaches and other earth tones.

- » **Sacred Space.** Create a special, calm space for meditation, journal writing, and yoga.

- » **Play soothing nature sounds.** Play natural sounds such as birds chirping, rolling waves, mountain streams and gentle breezes. These help your heart rate slow down and calm your nerves.

Here is a very intriguing observation. While researching ways to increase happiness, I discovered Suzanne Kane's article, **15 Ways to Increase Your Happiness**[17]. Note some of the ways Ms. Kane mentions: connect with others, be grateful, be positive and see the best in every situation, create goals and practice mindfulness. Sound familiar? Practice the habits and mindsets listed above and create your Happy Luck and Go Happy Go Lucky.

CONCLUSION

MAKE TOMORROW YOUR LUCKY DAY

In answer to the age-old question, does luck exist? Yes, it does. It lives within us. In our attitudes, our efforts and our mindsets. It exists within our 'Yes, I can, attitude.'

Are there lucky people? Yes, there are. The lucky people are those who believe in luck, who believe they will succeed. The lucky ones are those who strive for what they want. They are in control of their habits. Many thriving folk are engaged in self-improvement activities, honing their knowledge and skills. Successful people are networking or attending seminars, seeking new information, and reading about the latest ideas. They are taking community college courses, signing up for free workshops, or attending evening classes. Those with wanderlust may be working their way around the world. Some may be working two or more jobs to pay down debt or start a business.

Everyone experiences bad luck, traumatizing and challenging life events. For the most part, it is how we handle these occurrences that makes all the difference. There are some unfortunate people for whom luck wasn't' there, people with life-threatening illnesses, parents who lost a child, those living in war-torn countries or countries where most of the population ekes out a subsistence living. Therefore, it is up to us, those given first world, wonderful opportunities, to fully make the most of our luck.

If your luck is still hiding under a cloverleaf, try changing your 'un.' Change from unhappy, unlucky and unable, to untried, unfolding, unknown and unexpected. Find the four-leaf clover within yourself.

> The best luck of all is the luck
> you make for yourself.
> DOUGLAS MACARTHUR

I hope there was something within these pages for everyone: young parents starting a family, fledgling entrepreneurs looking for an edge or people of all ages seeking to start afresh with healthy habits. Those aspiring to become leaders or Titans can build on the mindsets of today's innovators. Adventurous souls can challenge themselves with diverse travel opportunities. Visualization and Feng-Shui might stir passion in passionate souls who lean toward alternate, holistic lifestyles. Believe in your luck.

> It is a great piece of skill to know how to guide
> your luck even while waiting for it.
> BALTASAR GRACIAN

Since we started with names, we will finish with names. As Dr. Seuss wrote in his final book, ***"Oh, The Places You'll Go!"***

You have brains in your head

You have feet in your shoes

You can steer yourself any direction you choose

So…be your name Buxbaum or Bixby or Bray

or Mordecai Ali Van Allen O'Shea

you're off to Great Places

Today is your day!

Your mountain is waiting.

So…get on your way.

Good Luck.

NOTES

INTRODUCTION- GETTING STARTED ON YOUR LUCKY LIFE

1. Scottberg, Erin of Learnvest, "9 Famous People Who Will Inspire You to Scottberg, Erin of Learnvest, "9 Famous People Who Will Inspire You to Never Give Up", themuse.com.
2. Scottberg, Erin of Learnvest, "9 Famous People Who Will Inspire You to Scottberg, Erin of Learnvest, "9 Famous People Who Will Inspire You to Never Give Up", themuse.com.

CHAPTER 2- APPRECIATING YOUR LUCK

1. Brady, Krissy, "11 Benefits of Lemon Water You Didn't Know About", lifehack.org
2. Lee, Stephanie, 1/26/17, Keep a 'Jar of Awesome" to remind yourself to Celebrate Small Wins, lifehacker.com/keep-a-jar-of-awesome-to-remind-yourself-to celebrate-1791488244
3. Corley, Thomas, C. May 22, 2014, Happiness Habit #10-Practice Gratitude for One Month
4. Schnalbruch, Sarah, February 12, 2015, Being grateful for what you have now could make you richer in the future, businessinsider.com.
5. Kane, Libby, August 20, 2014, This psychologist's impressive presentation shows how materialism is eroding our happiness, businessinsider.com.
6. Emmons, Robert, "Why Gratitude is Good", Greater Good Magazine, November 16, 2010

7. Emmons, Robert, "Why Gratitude is Good", Greater Good Magazine, November 16, 2010
8. Barker, Eric, September 20, 2015, New Neuroscience Reveals 4 Rituals That Will Make You Happy, bakadesuyo.com. Retrieved from: https://www.bakadesuyo.com/2015/09/make-you-happy-2/

CHAPTER 3- IT'S ALL IN THE NAME

1. Friedlander, Jamie, "10 Ways Your Name Affects Your Life", success.com, March 11, 2016
2. Goudreau, Jenna, 13 "surprising ways your name affects your success", businessinsider.com, Aug. 5, 2015
3. Baer, Drake, "Here's Why Using Your Middle Initial Makes You Look Smarter", businessinsider.com, May 2, 2014
4. Nelson, LD, Simmons, JP, Moniker Maladies: when names sabotage success., 2007, Dec. 18
5. Pietras Emma, August 7 2014, Mirror.co.uk.

CHAPTER 4- HOW TO MAKE LADY LUCK SMILE UPON YOU

1. Warrell, Margie, Six Things Lucky People Do That Others Don't, forbes.com, mar 17, 2015
2. Wiseman, Richard, The Luck Factor, Hyperion, New York, New York, 2003
3. Guillebeau, Chris, June 14, 2018, Side Hustle School #530, "Stoner Culture" Emojis Roll Out $10,000/Month in Passive Income, Retrieved from: https://sidehustleschool.com/podcasts/

4. Wiseman, Richard, The Luck Factor, Hyperion, New York, New York, 2003
5. Corley, Thomas, Rich Habits: The Daily Success Habits of Wealthy Individuals, Langdon Street Press, 2009
6. Rapoport, Betsy, goodhousekeeping.com, Get Lucky: The Four Things You Need to Do to Make This Year Amazing, Dec 16, 2013
7. Goins, Jeff, goinswriter.com
8. Jayson DeMers, 6 Ways to Actually Increase Your Luck, inc.com, Mar 17, 2015
9. Branson, Richard, My top 10 quotes on risk, virgin.com, Retrieved from https://www.virgin.com/richard-branson/my-top-10-quotes-risk
10. Nicholl, Katie, 2013, Kate, The Future Queen, Weinstein Books, New York
11. Mycoskie, Blake, May 15, 2012, Start Something That Matters, Spiegel and Grau, Penguin Random House
12. Ferriss, Tim, The Tim Ferriss Show #249, How To Make a Difference and Find Your Purpose, June 28, 2017
13. Wong, Kristen, The Wild Wong, #426 Optimal Living Daily-Luck is Not the Opposite of Hard Work
14. DeMers, Jayson, 6 Ways to Actually Increase Your Luck, inc.com, Retrieved from https://www.inc.com/jayson-demers/6-ways-to-actually-increase-your-luck.html
15. Pathak, Dr. Manavi, Conscientiousness: A Successful Leadership Trait, Medium, January 21, 2017
16. Sundara, Rajan, Conscientiousness – A Key Leadership Trait, Linkedin.com, June 27, 2016
17. Wiseman, Richard, The Luck Factor, Hyperion, New York, New York, 2003

18. "Eleanor Rigby History", Retrieved from http://www.beatlesebooks.com/eleanor-rigby
19. University of Cambridge, Personal and Professional Development, ppd.admin.cam.ac.uk Retrieved from https://www.ppd.admin.cam.ac.uk/professional-development/mentoring-university-cambridge/types-mentoring
20. Rodz, Carolyn, 6 Benefits of Having a Mentor, fortune.com, February 15, 2015
21. Schiff, Ben, 5 Ways You Can Make Your Own Luck, linkedin.com, April 8, 2014
22. Grant, Adam, Finding the Hidden Value in Your Network, linkedin.com, June 17, 2013.
23. Achor, Shawn, The Happiness Advantage: The Seven Principles of Positive Psychology That Fuel Success and Performance at Work, September 14, 2010.
24. Bookbinder, Dave, Which Comes First-Success or Happiness? HuffingtonPost.com, November 22, 2016, updated November 8, 2017

CHAPTER 5- LUCKY HABITS

1. Corley, Thomas, Rich Habits: The Daily Success Habits of Wealthy Individuals, Langdon Street Press, 2009
2. Kane, Libby, May 23, 2014, 10 Ways Rich People Think Differently, businessinsider.com, Retrieved from http://www.businessinsider.com/ways-rich-people-think-differently-2014-5
3. Wood and Neal, A New Look at Habits, Duke University, 2006
4. Duhigg, Charles, The Power of Habit, Anchor Canada, 2014

CHAPTER 6- DISCOVERING THE LUCKY HABITS

1. Merle, Andrew, 17/7/2017, This is When Successful People Wake Up, huffingtonpost.com, Retrieved from: https://www.huffingtonpost.com/entry/this-is-when-successful-people-wake-up_us_596d17a3e4b0376db8b65a1a
2. Snyder, Benjamin, 2017, April 6, What 'Shark Tank' investor Barbara Corcoran does each morning to stay productive all day. Retrieved from CNBC.com
3. Ramirez, Amenda and Kravitz, Len, Ph.D., January 2107, Weight Training May Boost Brain Power, Harvard Women's Health Watch. Retrieved from The Journal of the American Geriatrics Society, October 24, 2106
4. Godman, Heidi, April 9, 2014, Regular exercise changes the brain to improve memory, thinking skills, Retrieved from https://www.health.harvard.edu/blog/regular-exercise-changes-brain-improve-memory-thinking-skills-201404097110
5. Dientsmann, Giovanni, Scientific Benefits of Meditation-76 Things You Might Be Missing Out On. Retrieved from Live and Dare, liveanddare.com
6. Fortune Editors, December 19, 2106, Why Tim Ferriss Believes Meditation Is the Key to Success. Retrieved from fortune.com
7. Babauta, Len, January 15, 2016, Meditation for Beginners: 20 Practical Tips for Understanding the Mind. Retrieved from https://zenhabits.net/meditation-guide
8. Weller, Chris, 9 of the most successful people share their reading habits, Business Insider. Retrieved from ib.tdtu.edu.vn

9. Hallett, Rachel, October 12, 2016, Want to Live Longer? Read a Book. World Economic Forum. Retrieved from weforum.org
10. DesMarais, Christina, March 15, 2018, Why Reading Books Should be Your Priority, According to Science. Retrieved from Inc.com
11. Merle, Andrew, April 4, 2016, updated December 6, 2017, The Reading Habits of Ultra-Successful People. Retrieved from huffingtonpost.com
12. Perrin, Andrew, November 23, 2016, Who doesn't read books in America? Retrieved from http://www.pewresearch.org/fact-tank/2018/03/23/who-doesnt-read-books-in-america/.
13. McCraven, U.S. Navy Adm. William H. Retrieved from a commencement speech given at the University of Texas, May 16, 2014
14. Duhigg, Charles, The Power of Habit, Anchor Canada, 2014
15. Merle, Andrew, August 24, 2015, updated December 6, 2017, Make Your Bed, Change Your Life. Retrieved from https://www.huffingtonpost.com/andrew-merle/benefits-of-making-your-bed_b_7980354.html
16. Montag, Ali, December 4, 2017, Why 'Shark Tank investor Kevin O'Leary refuses to spend $2.50 on a cup of coffee. Retrieved from https://www.cnbc.com/2017/12/04/kevin-oleary-wont-pay-2-point-50-for-coffee-instead-he-invests-it.html
17. Bell, Randall, April 7, 2017, 7 'Rich Habits of Highly Successful People'. Retrieved from https://www.cnbc.com/2017/04/07/7-rich-habits-of-highly-successful-people.html
18. Locke, Robert, Why People Who Take Notes All the Time Are More Likely to Be Successful, Retrieved from https://

www.lifehack.org/298313/10-reasons-why-note-takers-are-the-fast-track-success

19. Nguyen, Thai, 02/13/2015, 10 Surprising Benefits You'll Get from Keeping a Journal. Retrieved from https://www.huffingtonpost.com/thai-nguyen/benefits-of-journaling-_b_6648884.html

20. Wiseman, Richard, The Luck Factor, Hyperion, New York, New York, 2003

21. Frank, Robert H., May 2016, Why Luck Matters More Than You Think. Retrieved from https://www.theatlantic.com/magazine/archive/2016/05/why-luck-matters-more-than-you-might-think/476394/.

22. Scott, Elizabeth, May 28, 2017, How To Use a Coincidence Journal to Increase Your Experience of Luck: Notice the Lucky Coincidences in Your Life. Retrieved from verywellmind.com, https://www.verywellmind.com/coincidence-journal-route-to-luck-3144669

23. Henry, Alan, 3/9/14, Why You Should Keep a Journal (and How to Start Yours). Retrieved from https://lifehacker.com/why-you-should-keep-a-journal-and-how-to-start-yours-1547057185

24. Purcell, Maud, The Health Benefits of Journaling. Retrieved from https://psychcentral.com/lib/the-health-benefits-of-journaling/.

25. Corley, Tom, September 8, 2016, 16 Rich Habits-Your autopilot mode can make you wealthy or poor. Retrieved from https://www.success.com/article/16-rich-habits.

26. Macher, Ingrid, How Volunteering Can Improve Your Health, Retrieved from http://gethealthygethot.com/4865/how-volunteering-can-improve-your-health/.

27. Segal, Jeanne, Ph.D. and Robinson, Lawrence, March 2018, Volunteering and its Surprising Benefits, How Giving to Others Makes You Healthier and Happier. Retrieved from https://www.helpguide.org/articles/healthy-living/volunteering-and-its-surprising-benefits.htm
28. Attachmentparenting.org, February 17, 2016, Kindness is Contagious
29. Fitzpatrick, Kelly, 08/11/2014, Updated Feb 07, 2017, 13 Tips for the Best Nap Ever, Huffington Post. Retrieved from https://www.huffingtonpost.com/2014/08/11/best-nap-napping-tips_n_5648651.html.
30. CBS News, Inside Google Workplaces, from perks to nap pods, Retrieved from https://www.cbsnews.com/news/inside-google-workplaces-from-perks-to-nap-pods/.
31. National Sleep Foundation, Napping, https://sleepfoundation.org/sleep-topics/napping.
32. Pink, Daniel, When: The Scientific Secrets of Perfect Timing, Riverhead Books, New York, 2018.

CHAPTER 7- HEALTHY BODY, HEALTHY MIND, HEALTHY BANK ACCOUNT

1. 39 Scientific Brain Benefits of Exercise, Retrieved from http://thebrainflux.com/brain-benefits-of-exercise/#section1
2. 39 Scientific Brain Benefits of Exercise, Retrieved from http://thebrainflux.com/brain-benefits-of-exercise/#section
3. Godman, Heidi, April 09, 2014, updated April 05, 2018, Regular exercise changes the brain to improve memory, thinking skills, Harvard Health Blog, Retrieved from https://www.health.harvard.edu/blog/regular-exercise-changes-brain-improve-memory-thinking-skills-201404097110

4. Suzuki, Wendy, The brain-changing benefits of exercise, TedWomen, 2017.
5. Hobson, Katherine, June 22, 2016, The Financial Rewards of Working Out, time.com, Retrieved from http://time.com/money/4368659/financial-rewards-working-out/.
6. 39 Scientific Brain Benefits of Exercise, thebrainflux.com, Retrieved from http://thebrainflux.com/brain-benefits-of-exercise/#section1
7. Breene, Sophia, October 7, 2013, 13 Unexpected Benefits of Exercise, greatist.com, Retrieved from https://greatist.com/fitness/13-awesome-mental-health-benefits-exercise.
8. Gladwell, Malcolm, Outliers, The Story of Success, Little, Brown and Company, Hatchette Book Group, New York, NY.
9. The Cognitive Benefits of Exercise, thebrainflux.com, Retrieved from http://thebrainflux.com/cognitive-benefits-exercise/.
10. Joe Verghese, M.D., Richard B. Lipton, M.D., Mindy J. Katz M.P.H., Charles B. Hall, Ph.D., June 19, 2013, Leisure Activities and the Risk of Dementia in the Elderly, nejm.org. Retrieved from http://www.nejm.org/doi/full/10.1056/NEJMoa022252.
11. Powers, Richard, July 30, 2010, Use It or Lose It: Dancing Makes You Smarter, Longer, socialdance.stanford.edu, Retrieved from, https://socialdance.stanford.edu/syllabi/smarter.htm.
12. Sifferlin, Alexandria, April 26, 2017, The Simple Reason, Exercise Enhances Your Brain. Retrieved from http://time.com/4752846/exercise-brain-health/.

13. Wheeling, Kate, May 31, 2017, This is Your Brain on Exercise, Outside Online, Retrieved from https://www.outsideonline.com/2186146/your-brain-exercise.
14. Godman, Heidi, April 09, 2014, Regular exercise changes the brain to improve memory, thinking skills-Harvard Health Blog, Retrieved from https://www.health.harvard.edu/blog/regular-exercise-changes-brain-improve-memory-thinking-skills-201404097110.

CHAPTER 8- OLD HABITS DO DIE HARD

1. Eurich, Tasha, Ph.D., 01/01/2014, The Science Behind Successful New Year's Resolutions, thehuffingtonpost.com, Retrieved from https://www.huffingtonpost.com/tasha-eurich-phd/new-years-resolutions_b_4512944.html.
2. Venkatraman, Rohini, Want to Actually Keep Your New Year's Resolution? Follow These 6 Science-Backed Steps, inc.com, Retrieved from https://www.inc.com/rohini-venkatraman/this-6-step-method-is-secret-to-a-new-years-resolution-that-lasts.html.

CHAPTER 9- TEAM LUCK-GOAL SETTING

1. Robbins, Tony, How Can I Create a Compelling Future?, Robbins Research International, Inc.
2. Godin, Seth, January 8, 2009, The thing about goals, typepad.com, Retrieved from http://sethgodin.typepad.com/seths_blog/2009/01/index.html.
3. Tracy, Brian, Positive Affirmations and Long-Term Goals Change Your Luck, www.briantracy.com, https://www.

briantracy.com/blog/personal-success/positive-affirmations-long-term-goals-goal-setting-self-improvement.

4. Matthews, Gail, Study focuses on strategies for achieving goals, resolutions, Dominican.edu., Retrieved from https://www.dominican.edu/dominicannews/study-highlights-strategies-for-achieving-goals.

5. Emmons, Robert, Ph. D. Gratitude and Well-Being, emmons.faculty.ucdavis.edu.

6. Niles, Frank, Ph.D., 6/17/2011, How to Use Visualization to Achieve Your Goals, huffingtonpost.com, https://www.huffingtonpost.com/frank-niles-phd/visualization-goals_b_878424.html.

7. Draznin, Hayley, Spanx founder: It's fun to make money- and to give it away, money, cnn.com., Retrieved from http://money.cnn.com/2017/05/05/smallbusiness/sara-blakely-spanx/index.html

8. Feloni, Richard, July 26, 2017, businessinsider.com.

CHAPTER 10- ARE WE BORN LUCKY?

1. Webber, Rebecca, May 1, 2010, Make Your Own Luck, Five principles for making the most of life's twists and turns, psychologytoday.com, Retrieved from https://www.psychologytoday.com/ca/articles/201005/make-your-own-luck

2. news.bbc.co.uk, 14 april 2004, Retrieved from http://news.bbc.co.uk/2/hi/health/3622817.stm

3. Han, Yu, Loria, Kevin, Sep. 1, 2016, scientists figured out how the month you are born in is linked to your health, businessinsider.com, Retrieved from http://www.businessinsider.com/birth-month-disease-risk-health-2016-8

4. Kluger, Jeffrey, April 17, 2017, How the Month You Were Born Affects Your Personality, According to Science, time.com, Retrieved from http://time.com/4741094/season-birth-personality/
5. Gladwell, Malcolm, October 29, 2008, Outliers: The Story of Success, Little Brown and Company
6. Flam, Faye, December 22, 2016, If You're So Smart, Why Aren't You Rich? Bloomberg LP, Retrieved from https://www.bloomberg.com/view/articles/2016-12-22/if-you-re-so-smart-why-aren-t-you-rich
7. Phelps, Michael, December 8, 2009, No Limits: The Will to Succeed, Free Press, page 67.
8. Brodwin, Erin, August 10, 2016, There's a huge misconception about how Olympic gymnasts like Simone Biles get their bodies, businessinsider.com, Retrieved from http://www.businessinsider.com/how-olympic-gymnasts-simone-biles-get-their-bodies-2016-8
9. McMahon, Daniel, July 26, 2016, After Chris Froome cut back on carbs for more protein, he lost twenty pounds, started winning the Tour de France, and became a millionaire
10. Phelps, Michael: Beneath the Surface, January 1, 2005, Sports Publishing LLC, page 281
11. Fisher, Max, April 17, 2012, Why Kenyans Make Such Great Runners: A Story of Genes and Cultures, theatlantic.com, Retrieved from https://www.theatlantic.com/international/archive/2012/04/why-kenyans-make-such-great-runners-a-story-of-genes-and-cultures/256015/

CHAPTER 11- GOOD LUCK OR BAD LUCK

1. Robehmed, Natalie, August 25, 2016, forbes.com, Retrieved from https://www.forbes.com/sites/natalierobehmed/2016/08/25/the-worlds-highest-paid-actors-2016-the-rock-leads-with-knockout-64-5-million-year/#3daa67c675a9
2. Umoh, Ruth, 11 Aug 2017, The Rock: This was the 'best thing that never' happened to me, cnbc.com, Retrieved from https://www.cnbc.com/2017/08/11/the-rock-this-was-the-best-thing-that-never-happened-to-me.html
3. Walker, Ruth, Sir Paul Smith, November 10, 2013, on becoming a designer by accident, scotsman.com, Retrieved from https://www.scotsman.com/lifestyle/culture/fashion/sir-paul-smith-on-becoming-a-designer-by-accident-1-3181723
4. Rubin, Gretchen, March 12, 2018, A Little Happier: Sometimes, You Have to Get Fired to Get Hired, gretchenrubin.com, Retrieved from https://gretchenrubin.com/podcast-episode/little-happier-fired-hired
5. Alexander Fleming, December 5, 2017, sciencehistory.org, Retrieved from https://www.sciencehistory.org/historical-profile/alexander-fleming
6. The Editors of Publications International, 9 Things Invented or Discovered by Accident, science.howstuffworks.com
7. Osmond, Kaetlyn, Feb.23, 2018 Canadian Winner Bronze Medal, Women's Figure Skating, 2018 Olympics, Castanet.net
8. Eikins, Kathleen, 31 Jan 2017, CNBC, Retrieved from https://www.cnbc.com/2017/01/31/hbs-rejection-was-the-best-thing-that-ever-happened-to-warren-buffett.html

9. Frank, Robert, 16 October 2013, Billionare Sara Blakely says secret to success is failure, cnbc.com, Retrieved from https://www.cnbc.com/2013/10/16/billionaire-sara-blakely-says-secret-to-success-is-failure.html
10. Sicinski, Adam, How to Attract the Good Luck You Need to Achieve Your Goals, blog.iqmatrix.com, Retrieved from https://blog.iqmatrix.com/attract-good-luck
11. designluck.com, Pablo Picasso: Harnessing Willpower, Retrieved from https://www.designluck.com/pablo-picasso-willpower/
12. Nel, Philip, Seussville.com, 2010

CHAPTER 12- EARTH LUCK-FENG SHUI-A LUCKY SECRET?

1. Man On (Mo) Wong, September 14 2016, The Truth About Feng Shui and Its Power, powerofinvisible.com., Retrieved from https://www.powerofinvisible.com/feng-shui/the-truth-about-feng-shui-and-its-power/
2. Rodika, Tchi, 10/03/17, The Spruce, Can Feng Shui Make Your Lucky?,
3. Rodika, Tchi, 10/03/17, The Spruce, Can Feng Shui Make Your Lucky?,
4. Fabrega, Marelisa, 20 Ways to Feel Wealthy, Lucky and Successful, daringtolivefully.com, Retrieved from https://daringtolivefully.com/wealthy-lucky-and-successful
5. The Delicious Day, Aug 13, 2104 Feng Shui Your Home For a Job You Love: 8 Steps. Retrieved from www.deliciousday.com/minimalism-2/feng-shui-for-career-job
6. S.BS. Surendran, Power of Underwater Shells and Conch, The Bali Times, March 23, 2015

7. Rodika, Tchi, 1/11/18, Lucky Bamboo Meaning and Use for Good Feng Shui, the spruce.com, Retrieved from https://www.thespruce.com/lucky-bamboo-use-for-good-feng-shui-1274635
8. Venkat, Nithya, December 14, 2017, Facts About the Lucky Bamboo Plant, dengarden, Retrieved from https://dengarden.com/gardening/What-is-Lucky-Bamboo-Facts-about-Lucky-Bamboo
9. S.BS. Surendran, Power of Underwater Shells and Conch, The Bali Times, March 23, 2015
10. Man On (Mo) Wong, September 14, 2016, The Truth About Feng Shui and its Power, powerof invisible.com, `https://www.powerofinvisible.com/feng-shui/the-truth-about-feng-shui-and-its-power/

CHAPTER 13- LUCKY CHARMERS

1. Wen, Tiffanie, 28 June 2017, The tricks to make yourself effortlessly charming, bbc.com., Retrieved from http://www.bbc.com/capital/story/20170627-the-tricks-to-make-yourself-effortlessly-charming
2. Schafer, Jack, Ph.D., Karlin, Marvin, Ph.D., January 13, 2015, The Like Switch, Simon and Schuster,
3. Clark, Dorie, as reported by Ella Banks, The Secrets to Starting Meetings in Your Favor, The Art of Charm Blog, Retrieved from https://theartofcharm.com/art-of-business/first-meeting-email-strategy/
4. Bradberry, Travis, January 27, 2015, 13 Habits of Exceptionally Likable People, forbes.com, Retrieved from: https://www.forbes.com/sites/travisbradberry/2015/01/27/13-habits of exceptionally-likeable-people//#6394dde51b1

CHAPTER 14- LUCKY CHARMS

1. Damisch, Lysann, Stoberock, Barbara, and Mussweiler, Thomas, 2/13/09, Keep Your Fingers Crossed! How Superstition Improves Performance, scribd.com, https://www.scribd.com/document/353089895/Lucky-Charms-Work-Research-Report-From-Cologne
2. Ossala, Alexandra, 2015, March 17 Popular Science, popsci.com, Retrieved from https://www.popsci.com/luck-real
3. Damisch, Lysann, Stoberock, Barbara, Mussweiler, Thomas, 2010, May 28, Keep Your Fingers Crossed! How Superstition Improves Performance, journals.sagepub.com
4. Zhang, Maggie, 2014, July 10, Why Your Superstitions Can Actually Help You, businessinsider.com
5. Vyse, Stuart, 2014, July 10, Why Your Superstitions Might Actually Be Good For You, businessinsider.com
6. Grauschopf, Sandra, 2017, June 21, thebalance.com
7. Ronca, Debra, Why are horseshoes considered to be lucky?" 18 August 2015.HowStuffWorks.com. <https://people.howstuffworks.com/horseshoes-lucky.htm> 7 April 2018

CHAPTER 15- LUCKY TRAVEL

1. Nguyen, Thai, 06/09/2016, 10 Proven Ways to Grow Your Brain: Neurogenisis and Neuroplasticity, huffingtonpost.com., Retrieved from https://www.huffingtonpost.com/thai-nguyen/10-proven-ways-to-grow-yo_b_10374730.html
2. Scott, Elizabeth, February 6, 2018, Vacations Are Important for More Than Just Fun, verywellmind.com, Retrieved from https://www.verywellmind.com/take-vacations-for-stress-relief-overall-health-3145274

3. Alton, Larry, May 19, 2017, 5 Scientifically Proven Health Benefits of Traveling Abroad, nbc.com, Retrieved from https://www.nbcnews.com/better/wellness/5-scientifically-proven-health-benefits-traveling-abroad-n759631
4. Alton, Larry, May 19, 2017, 5 Scientifically Proven Health Benefits of Traveling Abroad, nbc.com, Retrieved from https://www.nbcnews.com/better/wellness/5-scientifically-proven-health-benefits-traveling-abroad-n759631

CHAPTER 16- HAPPY GO LUCKY

1. Allan, Patrick, 9/14/15, What Researcher Says Happiness Really Is, Lifehacker.com, Retrieved from https://lifehacker.com/what-research-says-happiness-really-is-1730503184
2. Salmonsohn, Karen, June 30, 2011, The No. 1 Contributor to Happiness, psychologytoday.com, Retrieved from https://www.psychologytoday.com/intl/blog/bouncing-back/201106/the-no-1-contributor-happiness
3. Barker, Eric, July 23, 2014, Here's the schedule very successful people follow every day, theweek.com, http://theweek.com/articles/445444/heres-schedule-successful-people-follow-every-day
4. Holmes, Lindsey, December 21, 2106, Why We Love Listening to Sad Music on Repeat, Huffpost, https://www.huffingtonpost.ca/entry/why-we-like-sad-music_us_562a52a8e4b0aac0b8fc9e99
5. Landau, Elizabeth, February 10, 2009, Experiences Make Us Happier Than Possessions, Retrieved from http://www.cnn.com/2009/HEALTH/02/10/happiness.possessions/
6. McConnell, Allen, Ph.D., July 11, 2011, Friends with Benefits: Pets Make Us Happier, Healthier, Psychology Today, Retrieved

from https://www.psychologytoday.com/intl/blog/the-social-self/201107/friends-benefits-pets-make-us-happier-healthier
7. Harvard Health Publishing, November 2017, The pursuit of happiness, health.harvard.edu., https://www.health.harvard.edu/staying-healthy/the-pursuit-of-happiness
8. Harvard Health Publishing, November 2017, The pursuit of happiness, health.harvard.edu., https://www.health.harvard.edu/staying-healthy/the-pursuit-of-happiness
9. Wildnerness.org, September 30, 2014, Study: nature walks reduce stress, make us happier, Retrieved from https://wilderness.org/blog/study-nature-walks-reduce-stress-make-us-happier
10. Wildnerness.org, March 11, 2014, Time Magazine names nature as No. 1 way to improve your life, Retrieved from https://wilderness.org/blog/time-magazine-names-nature-1-way-improve-your-life
11. Emmons, Robert, June 1, 2007, Pay It Forward, greatergood.berkerley.edu.
12. Shanks, Nia, February 3, 2016, The Dirty Little Secret About Motivation, Purposeful Driven Living & Setting Goals, niashanks.com, Retrieved from http://www.niashanks.com/dirty-secret-motivation/
13. Dahl, Melissa, March 18, 2015, , Keep a One-Sentence Journal, Be Happier, The Cut
14. Clifford, Catherine, January 9, 2017, Tim Ferriss: 3 things you should do everyday if you want to be successful, cnbc.com, Retrieved from https://www.cnbc.com/2017/01/09/tim-ferriss-reveals-his-top-3-must-have-daily-habits.html
15. Segal, Jeanne, Ph.D. and Robinson, Lawrence, March 2018, Volunteering and its Surprising Benefits, How Giving

to Others Makes You Healthier and Happier, Retrieved from https://www.helpguide.org/articles/healthy-living/volunteering-and-its-surprising-benefits.htm
16. Braverman, Jody, October 27, 2016, 9 Feng-Shui Tips to Make You Healthier and Happier, livestrong.com, Retrieved from https://www.livestrong.com/slideshow/1011458-9-feng-shui-tips-make-healthier-happier/#slide=9
17. Kane, Suzanne, October 56, 2017, 15 Ways to Increase Your Happiness, psychcentral.com, Retrieved from https://psychcentral.com/lib/15-ways-to-increase-your-happiness/

ACKNOWLEDGEMENTS

> You don't have to justify a beautiful stroke of good luck. Accept it. Smile and say thank you.
>
> GARRISON KEILLOR, Pilgrims

Thank you to Michel and Blaise for their encouragement, advice and technical support. To Marie, special gratitude for her additional technical skill and assistance.

To the West Kelowna Writers' Group, thank you for making me realize writing a book was possible.

Wishing You Good Luck

ABOUT THE AUTHOR

Jamie believes luck is in all of us. She strives to enhance her lucky mindset. Jamie, open to new, lucky opportunities, has lived, worked and traveled throughout Canada, the United States, Africa, and South America. Unique activities intrigue Jamie and she has volunteered in Canada, Central America and Cambodia. Jamie worked in the educational field at a teacher, consultant and administrator. Currently living a lucky life on a lake, the author cultivates good habits and fills her gratitude journal.

You can connect with Jamie at:

jamiecmchugh@gmail.com or www.thebestofluck.biz